# Fresh Ways
# with Breakfasts & Brunches

Time-Life Books Inc.
is a wholly owned subsidiary of
**TIME INCORPORATED**

FOUNDER: Henry R. Luce 1898-1967

*Editor-in-Chief:* Henry Anatole Grunwald
*Chairman and Chief Executive Officer:* J. Richard Munro
*President and Chief Operating Officer:* N. J. Nicholas Jr.
*Chairman of the Executive Committee:*
Ralph P. Davidson
*Corporate Editor:* Ray Cave
*Executive Vice President, Books:* Kelso F. Sutton
*Vice President, Books:* George Artandi

*COVER*
*Spring sets the theme for a light brunch that celebrates the arrival of the season with cold tomato-and-orange soup, scallop-and-salmon sausages, salad and a fruit-and-meringue dessert (recipes, pages 108-111).*

## TIME-LIFE BOOKS INC.

EDITOR: George Constable
*Executive Editor:* Ellen Phillips
*Director of Design:* Louis Klein
*Director of Editorial Resources:* Phyllis K. Wise
*Editorial Board:* Russell B. Adams Jr., Dale M. Brown, Roberta Conlan, Thomas H. Flaherty, Lee Hassig, Donia Ann Steele, Rosalind Stubenberg, Kit van Tulleken, Henry Woodhead
*Director of Photography and Research:*
John Conrad Weiser

PRESIDENT: Christopher T. Linen
*Chief Operating Officer:* John M. Fahey Jr.
*Senior Vice Presidents:* James L. Mercer, Leopoldo Toralballa
*Vice Presidents:* Stephen L. Bair, Ralph J. Cuomo, Neal Goff, Stephen L. Goldstein, Juanita T. James, Hallett Johnson III, Robert H. Smith, Paul R. Stewart
*Director of Production Services:* Robert J. Passantino

Editorial Operations
*Copy Chief:* Diane Ullius
*Editorial Operations Manager:* Caroline A. Boubin
*Production:* Celia Beattie
*Quality Control:* James J. Cox (director)
*Library:* Louise D. Forstall

Correspondents: Elisabeth Kraemer-Singh (Bonn); Maria Vincenza Aloisi (Paris); Ann Natanson (Rome).

**Library of Congress Cataloguing in Publication Data**
Main entry under title:
Fresh ways with breakfasts & brunches.
    (Healthy home cooking)
    Includes index.
    1. Breakfasts. 2. Brunches. I. Time-Life Books. II. Title: Fresh ways with breakfasts and brunches. III. Series.
TX733.F74 1987    641.5'2    87-490
ISBN 0-8094-5852-7
ISBN 0-8094-5853-5 (lib. bdg.)

For information on and a full description of any Time-Life Books series, please write:
Reader Information
Time-Life Books
541 North Fairbanks Court
Chicago, Illinois 60611

Time-Life Books Inc. offers a wide range of fine recordings, including a *Rock 'n' Roll* series. For subscription information, call 1-800-445-TIME, or write TIME-LIFE MUSIC, Time & Life Building, Chicago, Illinois 60611.

## HEALTHY HOME COOKING

SERIES DIRECTOR: Dale M. Brown
*Series Administrators:* Jane Edwin, Elise Ritter Gibson
*Designer:* Tom Huestis
*Picture Editor:* Sally Collins
*Photographer:* Renée Comet
*Editorial Assistant:* Rebecca C. Christoffersen

Editorial Staff for *Fresh Ways with Breakfasts & Brunches:*
*Book Managers:* Jean Getlein, Barbara Sause
*Associate Picture Editor:* Scarlet Cheng
*Assistant Designer:* Elissa E. Baldwin
*Researcher/Writers:* Henry Grossi, Susan Stuck
*Copy Coordinators:* Elizabeth Graham, Ruth Baja Williams
*Picture Coordinator:* Linda Yates
*Photographer's Assistant:* Mazyar Parvaresh
*Kitchen Assistant:* Chhomaly Sok

*Special Contributors:* Mary Jane Blandford and Paula S. Rothberg (food purchasing), Sarah Brash (text), Peter Brett (recipe development and styling), Denise Cassis and Rebecca Johns (research), Shirley Corriher (food chemistry), Jennifer B. Gilman (design), Carol Gvozdich (nutrient analysis), Nancy Lendved (props), CiCi Williamson (microwave section).

## THE COOKS

LISA CHERKASKY has worked as a chef at numerous restaurants in Washington, D.C., and in Madison, Wisconsin, including nationally-known Le Pavillon and Le Lion d'Or. A graduate of The Culinary Institute of America at Hyde Park, New York, she has also taught classes in French cooking technique.

ADAM DE VITO began his cooking apprenticeship at L'Auberge Chez François near Washington, D.C., when he was only 14. He has worked at Le Pavillon restaurant, taught with cookbook author Madeleine Kamman and conducted classes at L'Académie de Cuisine in Maryland.

JOHN T. SHAFFER is a graduate of The Culinary Institute of America. He has had broad experience as a chef, including five years at The Four Seasons Hotel in Washington, D.C., where he was *chef saucier* at Aux Beaux Champs restaurant.

## THE CONSULTANT

CAROL CUTLER is the prizewinning author of many cookbooks; she also writes about food and entertaining for national magazines and newspapers. During the 12 years she lived in France, she studied at the Cordon Bleu and the École des Trois Gourmandes, as well as with private chefs. She is a member of the Cercle des Gourmettes, as well as a charter member and past president of Les Dames d'Escoffier.

## THE NUTRITION CONSULTANT

JANET TENNEY has been involved in nutrition and consumer affairs since she received her master's degree in human nutrition from Columbia University. She is the manager for developing and implementing nutritional programs for a major chain of supermarkets in the Washington, D.C., area.

Nutritional analyses for *Fresh Ways with Breakfasts & Brunches* were derived from Practorcare's Nutriplanner System and other current data.

*Other Publications:*

This volume is one of a series of illustrated cookbooks that emphasize the preparation of healthful dishes for today's weight-conscious, nutrition-minded eaters.

# *Fresh Ways*
# *with Breakfasts & Brunches*

BY

THE EDITORS OF TIME-LIFE BOOKS

TIME-LIFE BOOKS / ALEXANDRIA, VIRGINIA

# Contents

*Orange, Grapefruit and Honeydew Melon with Port*

*Chilled Papaya Shake*

*Turkey, Apple and Champagne Sausages*

*Chinese Brunch*

*Chewy Raisin and Nut Squares*

# Good Beginnings

The first meal of the day has an emotional aura quite unlike that of any other meal. Perhaps this springs from our peculiar vulnerability in the morning, when we still have sleep in our eyes and are feeling a little fuzzy, in need of gentle handling and a shock-free passage from the world of dreams into the world of reality. Presumably we also need nourishment to restore us after our long night's fast. The morning meal, more than lunch or dinner, reminds us of the essential function of food: to fuel our bodies.

When most Americans think of breakfast, just a handful of foods and beverages come to mind. These tend to be bland, safe, comfortingly familiar to the point of being boring: orange juice, grapefruit, bananas or prunes, eggs, cereals, bacon, ham or sausage, toast or muffins or pancakes, milk, coffee, tea. Europeans have their own everyday breakfast standbys: cheese, bread, ham, boiled eggs in Germany; croissants or bread and jam in France, served with a large cup of café au lait; eggs, kippers, fruit, rashers of bacon in England.

In many other parts of the world, breakfast is a far more eclectic affair. The Japanese think nothing of having soup upon arising. An Egyptian finds a bowl of beans as appropriate in the morning as in the evening. And a Chinese will happily down steamed or fried rice and a variety of dumplings, known as *dim sum* — "things that touch the heart."

Brunch — another, more elaborate way of breaking our daily fast — takes a liberalized approach to morning eating. A cross between breakfast and lunch, brunch piques imaginations — and appetites — because it is distinctly out of the ordinary daily routine. Timing alone makes brunch an innately festive meal: Usually meant to begin somewhere between 11 a.m. and 1 p.m., it is a meal for Sundays or holidays or the special Saturday when weekend chores are set aside and guests or family can be leisurely entertained.

This book takes its cue from brunch's freedom and reinvigorates morning eating with 131 original recipes. And it does so with your health in mind. It minimizes fats and salt, keeps protein in balance and maximizes fiber and complex carbohydrates, pres-

ent in fruits, grains and vegetables.

Although not all nutritionists believe that breakfast is actually a requirement for a healthful eating style, they generally agree that the meal is typically a matter of unhealthy extremes. There are many people, of course, who eat literally nothing for hours after arising; they effectively prolong the fast of the night to 12 or 15 hours or even longer. Some adults who follow this pattern get on quite well with their morning's activities. But for children, going without breakfast is another matter. Studies show that children who have had breakfast perform much better in school; they are less listless and can concentrate more effectively on their tasks.

In any case, eating a morning meal appears to make sound biological sense: Anthropologists think that our early ancestors were habitual nibblers who, in effect, ate many small meals through the day as they came upon edible berries, fruits or roots. Laboratory studies suggest that people may live longer when they eat three or more meals a day. Experiments with animals indicate that the animals fed one or two large meals gain twice as much body fat as those given the same number of calories divided among more frequent meals. Though the evidence is not clear-cut for humans, many nutritionists believe that eating breakfast does help control weight. Those persons who skip breakfast — or eat very little upon waking — may capitulate to fattening midmorning snacks or be so ravenous by lunchtime that they overeat.

Nutritionists recommend that breakfast provide a quarter of the day's calories — some 500 for the average woman and 675 for a man. By telescoping two meals into one, brunch can account for an even bigger bite — 800 calories for a woman and 1,080 for a man. The brunch menus and recipes in this volume have been developed to take these maximums into account, and to provide as much as 40 percent of the day's calories.

While most people do not skip breakfast, many eat a breakfast so bereft of nutrition that they need almost not bother. A sweet roll, consumed with a cup of coffee, will be high in calories, fat and sugar, to be sure, but fail to assuage appetite for long. Sugar's simple carbohydrates are quickly absorbed, and instead of a steady flow of energy to keep the body running smoothly through the morning, the level of blood sugar — the form in which energy is supplied to the body's cells — rises sharply to a peak, then declines rapidly, soon to be followed by a gnawing in the pit of the stomach. By contrast, complex carbohydrates are digested slowly, so that they provide a gradual and a sustained level of blood sugar that forestalls hunger.

At the opposite extreme is the traditional American breakfast. With its bacon, eggs, jams, egg-rich muffins and buttery breads, it is undesirably weighted with cholesterol, sugar and fat, as well as too much protein.

## Getting it right

Like lunch and dinner, the good breakfast should strike a balance among the different categories of food. Ideally, about 60 or 65 percent of breakfast's calories should come from complex carbohydrates, 5 percent from fats, another 10 percent from protein, and the remaining 5 percent or less from sugar, syrup or honey. Ounce for ounce, proteins and carbohydrates contain less than half the calories of fat.

Foods that are loaded with complex carbohydrates are said to be nutritionally dense, since they also contain vitamins, minerals and protein. Invariably these foods contain little or no fat. Often the little fat present is of the unsaturated variety that, unlike the saturated fat found in meat, eggs, milk, cream and cheese, has not been implicated in heart disease or other circulatory disorders.

Because they are such a rich source of complex carbohydrates, grains and vegetables are used frequently in the recipes making up this book. You will find these foods served up in tempting variations of traditional dishes, as well as in delicious innovations that can sway the most confirmed breakfast-hater.

## Breads of all kinds

No breakfast or brunch would be complete without bread in one form or another — yeast-raised loaves, unleavened flatbreads, muffins, dumplings, buns. Among the breads offered here, some are sweet, some savory, some baked, others steamed or cooked quickly on a griddle.

For sound health reasons, many of the recipes call for whole grains. Since these have been given only the lightest milling, just enough to strip the inedible outer husk from the kernel, they retain all three edible parts of the kernel: the fiber-rich jacket of bran; the starchy endosperm, which accounts for about 80 percent of the kernel's weight; and, enclosed by the endosperm, the germ. It is the germ that gives whole grains their distinctive,

rather nutty flavor, as well as their B and E vitamins and protein; the bran supplies the fiber.

Whole grains are marketed in a variety of forms. Groats are the coarsest — they are simply the whole kernel, minus its husk. Buckwheat, oats and wheat (somewhat inaccurately, the wheat groat is called a berry) can be purchased in groat form. Groats are also cracked or sliced into smaller pieces, or ground into flour or meal of varying degrees of fineness.

Because they retain the oil-laden germ, whole-grain products are much quicker to spoil than more highly refined products. All-purpose flour will keep up to six months at room temperature. Stored in a tightly covered container in the refrigerator, groats remain fresh for four or five months. The more finely textured products, including cracked wheat, meal and flour, are quicker to spoil. Buy them in small quantities, store them in the refrigerator, and plan to use them within three months.

Several of the breads in this book call for combinations of different flours. Where a light texture is desirable, it is essential to include a large proportion of flour milled from wheat. Only wheat contains a significant amount of gluten, the protein that gives bread its structure. All-purpose flour produces a lighter-textured bread than whole-wheat flour, whose germ and bran content interfere with the gluten's ability to develop fully. Bread flour has more gluten and creates a sturdier loaf.

Thorough kneading is essential to provide a yeast-leavened dough with good body. But quick breads, which generally are leavened by baking soda or baking powder, actually suffer if they are mixed too long or too vigorously. Baking soda and powder, like yeast organisms, release bubbles of carbon dioxide that cause dough to rise. But whereas yeast tends to work slowly, these agents go into action as soon as they are moistened. Consequently, quick bread batters or doughs should be mixed only long enough to combine the ingredients well — overmixing will drive out the carbon-dioxide bubbles.

Do not let a quick-bread dough or batter stand for long after mixing, since delaying cooking will allow the carbon dioxide to escape. Once the bread is done, serve it warm or as fresh as possible; it will not benefit from standing around any more than a pancake, a waffle or a popover would.

Keep your baking powder tightly covered and discard the unused portion no more than 12 months after purchase — otherwise you risk disappointing results. You can test baking powder's efficacy by adding one teaspoonful to one third cup of hot water. Few bubbles mean that the baking powder is past its prime.

The quick breads most closely identified with breakfast and brunch are pancakes, waffles, crepes and French toast. As conventionally prepared, they tend to be high in calories, fat and cholesterol; for this book, they have all been redesigned to fit a healthier mold. Egg yolks have been reduced in the recipes (a

## The Key to Better Eating

Healthy Home Cooking addresses the concerns of today's weight-conscious, health-minded cooks with recipes that take into account guidelines set by nutritionists. The secret to eating well, of course, has to do with maintaining a balance of foods in the diet. The recipes thus should be used thoughtfully, in the context of a day's eating. To make the choice easier, this book presents an analysis of nutrients in a single serving of each breakfast or brunch recipe, as in the breakdown at right. The counts for calories, protein, cholesterol, total fat, saturated fat and sodium are approximate.

### Interpreting the chart

The chart below shows the National Research Council's Recommended Dietary Allowances of calories and protein for healthy men, women and children, along with the council's recommendations for the "safe and adequate" maximum intake of sodium. Although the council has not established recommendations for either cholesterol or fat, the chart does include what the National Institutes of Health and the American Heart Association consider the daily maximum amounts of these for healthy members of the general population.

The volumes in the Healthy Home Cooking series do not purport to be diet books, nor do they focus on health foods. Rather, they express a commonsense approach to cooking that uses salt, sugar, cream, butter and oil in moderation while employing other ingredients that also provide flavor and satisfaction. Herbs, spices and aromatic vegetables, as well as fruits, peels, juices, wines and vinegars are all used toward this end.

In this volume, both safflower oil and virgin olive oil are often called for. Safflower oil was chosen because it is the most highly polyunsaturated vegetable fat commonly available in supermarkets, and polyunsaturated fats reduce blood cholesterol. Virgin olive oil is used because it has a fine fruity flavor that is lacking in the lesser grade

Calories **109**
Protein **14g.**
Cholesterol **32mg.**
Total fat **2g.**
Saturated fat **1g.**
Sodium **162g.**

known as "pure." In addition, virgin olive oil is — like all olive oil — high in monounsaturated fats, which do not increase blood cholesterol and, according to recent research, may even lower it. Some cooks, seeking a still fruitier flavor for their brunchtime salads, may wish to use extra virgin olive oil or even extra extra virgin, although to be sure the price will be higher, reflecting the quality of such an oil.

The recipes make few unusual demands. Naturally they call for fresh ingredients, offering substitutes when these are unavailable. (Only the original ingredient is calculated in the analysis, however.) Most of the ingredients can be found in any well-stocked supermarket. If whole grains are unavailable, look for them in a health food store. Any ingredients that may seem unusual are described in a glossary on pages 139 and 140.

In instances where particular techniques may be unfamiliar to a cook, there are appropriate how-to photographs.

In Healthy Home Cooking's test kitchens, heavy-bottomed pots and pans are used to guard against burning the food whenever a small amount of oil is used and when there is the danger that the food will adhere to the hot surface, but nonstick pans can be utilized as well.

### About cooking times

To help the cook plan ahead, Healthy Home Cooking takes time into account in its recipes. While recognizing that everyone cooks at a different speed, and that stoves and ovens differ, the series provides approximate "working" and "total" times for every dish. Working time stands for the minutes actively spent on preparation; total time includes unattended cooking time, as well as time devoted to marinating or chilling ingredients. Since the recipes emphasize fresh foods, they may take a bit longer to prepare than "quick and easy" dishes that call for canned or packaged products, but the payoff in flavor, and often in nutrition, should compensate for the little extra time involved.

### Recommended Dietary Guidelines

| | | Average Daily Intake | | Maximum Daily Intake | | | |
|---|---|---|---|---|---|---|---|
| | | CALORIES | PROTEIN grams | CHOLESTEROL milligrams | TOTAL FAT grams | SATURATED FAT grams | SODIUM milligrams |
| Children | 7-10 | 2400 | 22 | 240 | 80 | 27 | 1800 |
| Females | 11-14 | 2200 | 37 | 220 | 73 | 24 | 2700 |
| | 15-18 | 2100 | 44 | 210 | 70 | 23 | 2700 |
| | 19-22 | 2100 | 44 | 300 | 70 | 23 | 3300 |
| | 23-50 | 2000 | 44 | 300 | 67 | 22 | 3300 |
| | 51-75 | 1800 | 44 | 300 | 60 | 20 | 3300 |
| Males | 11-14 | 2700 | 36 | 270 | 90 | 30 | 2700 |
| | 15-18 | 2800 | 56 | 280 | 93 | 31 | 2700 |
| | 19-22 | 2900 | 56 | 300 | 97 | 32 | 3300 |
| | 23-50 | 2700 | 56 | 300 | 90 | 30 | 3300 |
| | 51-75 | 2400 | 56 | 300 | 80 | 27 | 3300 |

single yolk suffices for four people) and egg whites increased, with results that are light, moist and tender. The commercial syrups and spreads ordinarily poured over these breads are replaced by homemade versions that are deliberately less sweet, yet full of natural fruit flavor. And fresh fruit is the basis of several delightful toppings.

The fat and caloric content of stovetop breads can be further reduced by the right choice of the pan or griddle. With a non-stick finish or, in the case of a cast-iron utensil, a well-seasoned cooking surface, only a trace of fat need be added to prevent the bread from sticking.

To season a cast-iron pan, cover its cooking surface with a flavorless vegetable oil. Place the pan in a 250° F. oven. After an hour, turn off the heat and leave the pan in the oven for 12 hours. When you remove the pan, wipe it with paper towels to remove any excess oil. To clean the pan after cooking without damaging the seasoning, simply rinse it with water, dry it and wipe it out lightly with a paper towel soaked with a little vegetable oil.

For most people, breakfast is not complete without a bracing cup of hot coffee or tea. Like the skillet or griddle, the coffee pot deserves special attention. Even if you eschew coffee in favor of tea, cocoa, fruit juice or some other morning beverage, there may be times when you will want to serve a well-made brew. Since bare metal can impart a bitter flavor to coffee, choose a pot made of glass or porcelain and clean it after every use with a solution of baking soda and water. (Soap or detergent may leave a residue or film.) And, whether you make coffee by drip, vacuum or percolator method, remove the grounds and serve the coffee immediately, or at the very latest, within a half hour of brewing it. If this is not possible, keep the coffee warm over gentle heat; never allow it to boil — boiling will only make it bitter.

## How this book works

The recipes in the first section are for both breakfast and brunch dishes — hot cereals, baked breads, stovetop breads, beverages, side dishes of fruits or vegetables, spreads, and main dishes based on eggs, grains, meat or seafood. Some of these are good candidates for workday breakfasts, such as the speedily prepared frozen peach, banana and buttermilk drink on page 23 that is practically a meal in a glass.

The second section of the book offers a series of brunch menus that include main dishes, salads, soups, side dishes, light desserts, breads and beverages. Some of the menus take their inspiration from a particular national or regional culinary tradition, while others reflect a seasonal theme. There is, as well, a menu for a simple picnic brunch and another for a buffet suitable for a dozen people.

The third and last section features microwave recipes. When time is short, a microwave oven can be a tremendous help in getting breakfast or brunch on the table fast.

And time is a key issue. It is the reason that so many people make do with a breakfast that is a skimpy, unsatisfying, rushed affair. With a little planning and organization, however, it is possible to have an appetizing, healthful meal in the morning. For some people, of course, getting organized shortly after rising is not within their nature. Time set aside the night before for a few chores will help speed up operations in the morning. Steps that can be taken in advance are:
- Set the table and get out the utensils you will need.
- Measure and combine all the dry ingredients for muffins, stovetop breads or quick breads; cover them tightly so that no flavors or aromas will escape.
- Mix liquid ingredients for pancakes, French toast or waffles; cover the containers tightly and refrigerate them.
- Oil baking tins.

Although brunch, by virtue of its later hour, allows more morning preparation time, it is still wise to do some of the work at least a day ahead:
- Cook crepes, stack them one upon the other between pieces of wax paper, wrap them tightly in foil and refrigerate them.
- Prepare frozen dishes such as sorbets or chilled ones such as gelatin salads and soups.
- Bake cookies and yeast breads. Most yeast breads actually benefit from being baked a day in advance, since their flavor will improve and their texture will become firmer, thus making them easier to slice.
- Cook and refrigerate seafood, covered, for use in salads or as filling for crepes.
- Prepare sauces, toppings and spreads.
- Mix marinades and refrigerate them.
- Cook the base for a soufflé and refrigerate it. The next day, heat it gently before adding the other ingredients.

With some of the work done in advance, you will have more of an opportunity to be with your guests and to enjoy with them a meal that is not only delicious but good for them.

*1 Sunlight greets a leisurely Sunday breakfast of scallion-and-rice muffins with apricot spread, a vegetable frittata and orange slices with pomegranate seeds.*

# Pleasures of Morning

Morning eating comes in many guises, and this section shows just how diverse and enjoyable it can be. You will find recipes for an array of breakfast and brunch dishes, some as predictable as pancakes (but with a difference), and other dishes as surprising as a vegetable-stuffed strudel *(page 83)*.

Because healthful eating means going easy on salt and fat, none of the prepared meats ordinarily linked with morning meals are included here. (Bacon alone consists of more than two thirds fat, and breakfast sausage is half fat.) Instead, the recipes use low-fat protein sources: fish, poultry, ricotta cheese, yogurt, and extra-lean cuts of beef and pork. Typical of this approach is a homemade sausage of ground turkey, delicately laced with Champagne to lend it a piquancy that more than makes up for the little salt used.

To give early-morning eating a boost, the recipes involve enticing blends of flavors. Buttermilk, fruit and spices enliven whole-grain hot cereals, whose innately richer taste needs less bolstering with salt than the blander refined cereals. Similarly, scallions, sage and dill bring a delightful accent to some of the other early-day dishes assembled here.

Fresh fruit has particular importance in morning menus. Frothy mixtures of fruit and milk make wonderful eye openers. Chopped and stirred into a batter for baked or stove-top breads, fruit satisfies the longing for something sweet at low-caloric cost. In addition, there are several fruit dishes that can be prepared in a matter of minutes and are as suitable for a weekend brunch as a workday breakfast. Rounding out the fruit recipes are a variety of toppings, syrups and relishes. These fruity fillips have multiple uses. For instance, the strawberry-cranberry jam that accompanies the main-dish turkey-cheese sandwich on page 68 is equally delicious paired with the orange French toast on page 63 or the cornmeal-buttermilk pancakes on page 61 — all dishes that should encourage you to rise and shine.

## Swiss Oatmeal

THE SWISS CEREAL KNOWN AS MUESLI, ON WHICH THIS
RECIPE IS BASED, GENERALLY CONTAINS DRIED FRUIT;
HERE FRESH FRUIT IS USED, AND THE CEREAL IS MOISTENED
WITH BOTH APPLE CIDER AND YOGURT.

Serves 6
Working (and total) time: about 10 minutes

Calories **160**
Protein **5g.**
Cholesterol **2mg.**
Total fat **3g.**
Saturated fat **0g.**
Sodium **29mg.**

| |
| --- |
| 1 red apple, quartered, cored and coarsely chopped |
| 1 yellow apple, quartered, cored and coarsely chopped |
| ½ cup apple cider or unsweetened apple juice |
| 1 cup quick-cooking rolled oats |
| 1 tbsp. honey |
| 1 cup plain low-fat yogurt |
| 2 tbsp. sliced almonds |
| 2 tbsp. raisins |
| 1 tbsp. dark brown sugar |

Put the chopped apples into a large bowl. Add the
cider or apple juice and toss the apples to moisten
them. Stir in the oats and honey, then add the yogurt,
almonds and raisins. Stir to combine the mixture well.
  Serve the Swiss oatmeal in individual bowls; sprinkle
each serving with ½ teaspoon of the brown sugar.

EDITOR'S NOTE: *If you wish, Swiss oatmeal can be made
ahead and kept in the refrigerator, covered with plastic wrap,
for up to two days.*

## Homemade Granola

WITH MILK ADDED, THIS GRANOLA BECOMES
A BREAKFAST IN ITSELF.

Serves 8
Working (and total) time: about 30 minutes

Calories **255**
Protein **6g.**
Cholesterol **0mg.**
Total fat **10g.**
Saturated fat **1g.**
Sodium **102mg.**

| |
| --- |
| 1 cup rolled oats |
| ½ cup wheat bran |
| ¼ cup untoasted sunflower seeds (about 1 oz.) |
| ½ cup whole blanched almonds (about 2 oz.) |
| 2 tbsp. sesame seeds |
| 2 tsp. safflower oil |
| ¼ tsp. salt |
| 1 cup raisins |
| 10 pitted dates, chopped |
| 2 tbsp. honey |
| 1 tsp. vanilla |
| grated zest of 1 orange |

Preheat the oven to 400° F. Combine the oats, bran,
sunflower seeds, almonds, sesame seeds, oil and salt
in a large bowl. Spread the mixture evenly on a jelly-
roll pan and toast it in the oven, stirring the mixture every five minutes, until it is lightly browned —
about 15 minutes.
  Return the toasted mixture to the bowl. Stir in the
raisins, dates, honey, vanilla and orange zest. Let the
granola cool completely before storing it in an airtight
container. Serve the granola in individual bowls, with
low-fat milk poured over it if you like.

# Apricot-Orange Breakfast Couscous

Serves 4
Working time: about 5 minutes
Total time: about 10 minutes

Calories **220**
Protein **6g.**
Cholesterol **0mg.**
Total fat **2g.**
Saturated fat **1g.**
Sodium **203mg.**

| |
|---|
| 1 cup fresh orange juice |
| 12 dried apricot halves, thinly sliced |
| ¼ tsp. salt |
| 1 cup couscous |
| 3 tbsp. unsweetened dried coconut |
| fresh fruit (optional) |
| low-fat milk (optional) |

Put the orange juice, 1 cup of water, all but 1 table-spoon of the apricots and the salt into a medium saucepan. Bring the mixture to a boil. Stir in the couscous and remove the pan from the heat; cover the pan and let it stand for five minutes.

Toast the coconut by putting it in a small, heavy-bottomed saucepan and cooking it, stirring constantly, until it is lightly browned — about five minutes. Spoon the couscous into individual serving bowls. Top each portion with some of the reserved tablespoon of sliced apricot and some coconut. You may garnish the hot cereal with fresh fruit such as raspberries, orange segments, or sliced pineapple or mango. Serve the cereal at once; accompany it with low-fat milk if you like.

## Apple-Cinnamon Breakfast Bulgur

Serves 4
Working time: about 5 minutes
Total time: about 20 minutes

Calories **208**
Protein **5g.**
Cholesterol **0mg.**
Total fat **1g.**
Saturated fat **0g.**
Sodium **137mg.**

| |
|---|
| *1 tart apple, preferably Granny Smith, cut in half and cored* |
| *1 cup plus 1 tbsp. apple cider or unsweetened apple juice* |
| *1 tbsp. currants or raisins* |
| *¼ tsp. ground cinnamon* |
| *¼ tsp. salt* |
| *1 cup bulgur* |
| *low-fat milk (optional)* |

Cut one half of the apple into thin slices. Put the apple slices into a small bowl and toss them with 1 tablespoon of the cider or apple juice. Set the bowl aside.

Cut the remaining apple half into small chunks. Put the chunks into a heavy-bottomed saucepan. Add the remaining cup of cider or apple juice, 1 cup of water, the currants or raisins, the cinnamon, and the salt, and bring the mixture to a boil. Stir in the bulgur, then cover the pan and reduce the heat to medium low. Simmer the bulgur mixture until all of the liquid is absorbed — about 15 minutes.

Spoon the bulgur into individual serving bowls and decorate each portion with some of the reserved apple slices. If you like, serve the cereal with low-fat milk.

# Toasted Brown-Rice Cereal with Orange and Cocoa

Serves 6
Working time: about 15 minutes
Total time: about 30 minutes

Calories **215**
Protein **3g.**
Cholesterol **0mg.**
Total fat **10g.**
Saturated fat **0g.**
Sodium **98mg.**

| |
|---|
| 1 cup brown rice |
| ¼ tsp. salt |
| 2 tbsp. unsweetened cocoa powder |
| ½ cup dark brown sugar |
| ½ cup fresh orange juice |
| 1 navel orange, peeled and cut into segments |

Toast the brown rice in a heavy-bottomed skillet over medium-high heat, shaking the pan occasionally, until the rice begins to crackle and some of the kernels start to burst — seven to 10 minutes. Transfer the rice to a blender and grind it until it resembles coarse sand.

Put the ground rice and salt into a saucepan; add 3 cups of cold water and bring the mixture to a simmer over medium-high heat. Reduce the heat to medium low, then cover the pan and cook the rice until all but about 1 cup of the water has been absorbed and the rice is tender — approximately 15 minutes. Remove the pan from the heat. Sift the cocoa onto the rice and then stir it in. Add the brown sugar and orange juice; stir the mixture well.

Spoon the cereal into warm bowls, then top each serving with several of the orange segments. Serve the cereal with low-fat milk, if you like.

## Multigrain Cereal Mix

THIS UNCOOKED CEREAL CAN BE AS VARIED OR SIMPLE AS YOU LIKE. YOU MAY LEAVE OUT ONE OR TWO OF THE GRAINS. MOST OF THE INGREDIENTS ARE READILY FOUND IN THE SUPERMARKET. THE RYE AND MILLET ARE AVAILABLE IN MOST HEALTH-FOOD STORES.

Makes about 16 servings
Working (and total) time: about 10 minutes

Calories **95**
Protein **3g.**
Cholesterol **0mg.**
Total fat **1g.**
Saturated fat **0g.**
Sodium **15mg.**

| |
|---|
| *1 cup puffed wheat* |
| *1 cup puffed rice* |
| *1 cup puffed corn* |
| *1 cup rolled oats* |
| *1 cup rolled rye or rye flakes* |
| *1 cup puffed millet or millet flakes* |
| *½ cup seedless raisins or currants* |
| *2 tbsp. chopped toasted almonds, hazelnuts or pecans* |

Combine the cereals in a large bowl. Stir in the raisins or currants and the nuts.

Store the cereal mix in an airtight container. If you wish, serve each portion with low-fat milk or yogurt.

EDITOR'S NOTE: *You may add ¼ cup of chopped, pitted dates or 1 tablespoon of toasted sesame seeds to this cereal. To toast the nuts or sesame seeds, put them into a heavy-bottomed skillet over medium-high heat and stir them constantly until they are lightly browned — two to three minutes.*

# Banana and Orange Oatmeal

Serves 4
Working (and total) time: about 10 minutes

Calories **193**
Protein **6g.**
Cholesterol **1mg.**
Total fat **2g.**
Saturated fat **0g.**
Sodium **17mg.**

| |
|---|
| 1 ⅓ cups fresh orange juice |
| 1 tsp. grated orange zest |
| 1 banana, peeled and coarsely chopped |
| 1 ⅓ cups quick-cooking rolled oats |
| ½ cup skim milk |
| 1 orange, peeled and segmented |

Combine the orange juice, orange zest and banana in a nonreactive saucepan and bring the mixture to a boil. Stir in the rolled oats, reduce the heat to low and cook the mixture, covered, for one minute. Take the pan from the heat and let the oatmeal stand, covered, until it has thickened — about one minute more.

Spoon the cereal into four individual bowls; add two tablespoons of the milk to each bowl and garnish it with one or two of the orange segments. Serve the oatmeal at once.

## Mixed Vegetable
## Eye Opener

Makes 2 servings
Working time: about 20 minutes
Total time: about 1 hour (includes chilling)

Calories **63**
Protein **3g.**
Cholesterol **0mg.**
Total fat **0g.**
Saturated fat **0g.**
Sodium **210mg.**

| |
|---|
| 2 celery stalks, trimmed, leaves reserved |
| 1 cucumber, peeled, seeded and coarsely chopped |
| 1½ tsp. fresh lemon juice |
| 8 drops hot red-pepper sauce |
| 14 oz. canned unsalted whole tomatoes, seeded, with their juice |
| ⅛ tsp. salt |
| ½ tsp. sugar |
| 2 scallions, trimmed, the white parts coarsely chopped, the green parts reserved for another use |
| ½ tsp. ground ginger |
| ¼ tsp. dill seeds (optional) |
| 1 carrot, quartered lengthwise, for garnish |

Remove the strings from the celery stalks using a vegetable peeler or a paring knife. Cut the stalks into 1-inch pieces and set them aside.

Place the cucumber, lemon juice and hot red-pepper sauce in a food processor or a blender; process the mixture until it is smooth. Add the celery pieces and purée the mixture. Add the tomatoes and their juice, the salt, sugar, scallions, ginger and ⅛ teaspoon of the dill seeds, if you are including them, and process the mixture, using short bursts, until it is smooth again.

Chill the mixture for at least 40 minutes. Pour the drink into glasses; sprinkle each serving with a few of the remaining dill seeds if you are using them, then float the reserved celery leaves on top. Insert one or two carrot sticks into each drink and serve.

EDITOR'S NOTE: *To frost the glasses, place them in the freezer for 30 minutes before serving the drink.*

## Chilled Papaya Shake

Makes 4 servings
Working (and total) time: about 15 minutes

Calories **86**
Protein **3g.**
Cholesterol **2mg.**
Total fat **1g.**
Saturated fat **0g.**
Sodium **67mg.**

| |
| --- |
| 1 ripe papaya (about 1 lb.), peeled, seeded and cut into chunks |
| 2 tsp. fresh lemon juice |
| ¼ tsp. ground allspice |
| ¾ cup fresh orange juice |
| 2 tsp. honey |
| 1 cup buttermilk |
| 4 ice cubes |
| lemon slices for garnish |

Put the papaya, lemon juice, ⅛ teaspoon of the all-spice, and about half of the orange juice into a blender or a food processor, and purée the mixture. Add the honey, buttermilk, the remaining orange juice and the ice, and blend the mixture until it is smooth — about 30 seconds in the blender or one minute in the processor.

To serve the papaya shake, pour it into glasses and sprinkle the drinks with some of the remaining allspice. Garnish each shake with a slice of lemon.

## Hot and Spicy Tomato Juice

Makes 4 servings
Working time: about 10 minutes
Total time: about 20 minutes

Calories **39**
Protein **2g.**
Cholesterol **0mg.**
Total fat **0g.**
Saturated fat **0g.**
Sodium **18mg.**

| |
| --- |
| 28 oz. canned unsalted whole tomatoes, puréed in a food processor or a blender and sieved |
| 3 tbsp. fresh lime juice |
| ⅛ tsp. ground cayenne pepper |
| 2 tbsp. chopped fresh mint |
| 4 lime slices, for garnish (optional) |

Combine the puréed tomatoes, lime juice, cayenne pepper and mint in a nonreactive saucepan. Heat the mixture over low heat and simmer it for 10 minutes. Garnish each serving with a slice of lime, if you like, and serve the drink hot.

# Raspberry Frappé

Makes 6 servings
Working time: about 20 minutes
Total time: about 1 hour and 45 minutes
(includes chilling)

Calories **132**
Protein **3g.**
Cholesterol **4mg.**
Total fat **1g.**
Saturated fat **1g.**
Sodium **31mg.**

| |
|---|
| *3 cups fresh orange juice* |
| *2 tbsp. instant tapioca* |
| *2 tbsp. sugar, if you are using fresh raspberries* |
| *2 cups fresh or frozen raspberries* |
| *1¼ cups low-fat milk* |

Put the orange juice into a nonreactive saucepan; stir in the tapioca and the sugar, if you are using it, and let the mixture stand for five minutes. Bring the liquid to a boil, stirring constantly. Remove the pan from the heat and let the mixture cool completely.

Add the raspberries and purée the mixture, one half at a time, in a blender or a food processor. Strain each batch through a fine sieve. Cover the purée with plastic wrap and chill it for at least one hour, then whisk in the milk. If you like, serve the frappé in chilled glasses.

# Banana-Peach Buttermilk Shake

Makes 2 servings
Working time: about 5 minutes
Total time: about 6 hours (includes freezing)

Calories **152**
Protein **5g.**
Cholesterol **5mg.**
Total fat **2g.**
Saturated fat **1g.**
Sodium **129mg.**

| |
|---|
| 1 large banana, peeled and sliced |
| 1 ripe peach, peeled, halved, pitted and sliced, or 1 cup frozen unsweetened sliced peaches |
| 1 cup buttermilk |
| ¼ cup fresh orange juice |

*2 strawberries for garnish (optional)*

Wrap the banana slices in plastic wrap and freeze them for at least six hours. If you are using fresh peach slices, wrap and freeze them at the same time.

When you are ready to prepare the shakes, put the banana and peach slices, the buttermilk and orange juice into a food processor or a blender; process the mixture until it is smooth — about one minute. Pour the purée into tall glasses. If you like, garnish each glass with a strawberry. Serve the shakes at once.

# Orange, Grapefruit and Honeydew Melon with Port

Serves: 8
Working (and total) time: about 40 minutes

| | |
|---|---|
| Calories **118** | *1 grapefruit* |
| Protein **1g.** | *2 navel oranges* |
| Cholesterol **0mg.** | *½ cup ruby port or Madeira* |
| Total fat **0g.** | *½ cup fresh orange juice* |
| Saturated fat **0g.** | *2 tbsp. light or dark brown sugar* |
| Sodium **18mg.** | *1 honeydew melon, seeded and peeled, the flesh cut into 8 wedges and chilled* |

Peel and segment the grapefruit and the oranges as demonstrated below, reserving the juices. Strain the juices into a small saucepan. Put the fruit in a bowl and refrigerate it while you make the sauce.

Add the port or Madeira, the ½ cup of orange juice and the sugar to the citrus juices in the saucepan, and bring the mixture to a boil. Reduce the heat to medium and simmer the liquid until it is reduced to about ½ cup — about 25 minutes. Let the sauce cool, then stir it into the fruit in the bowl.

Meanwhile, cut one wedge of honeydew melon in half crosswise, then into thin slices. Spread the slices in the shape of a fan on a chilled individual serving plate. Repeat the process with the remaining wedges. Spoon the citrus segments and the sauce over the melon fans and serve them at once.

## Segmenting a Citrus Fruit

**1** REMOVING THE ENDS. To obtain segments free of pith and membrane from a citrus fruit (here, a grapefruit), use a sharp, stainless-steel knife to slice off both ends of the fruit.

**2** CUTTING OFF THE PEEL. With the fruit standing on a flat end, slice off the peel in vertical strips, following the fruit's contour. Turn the fruit after each cut and continue to remove strips until peel and pith are entirely removed.

**3** FREEING THE SEGMENTS. Working over a bowl to catch the juices, hold the grapefruit in one hand and carefully slice between flesh and membranes to free each segment. Let the segments fall into the bowl as you detach them.

# Curried Fruit Compote

THIS DISH CAN BE SERVED AS A BREAKFAST ENTRÉE OR
A SIDE DISH ON A BRUNCH MENU.

Serves 6
Working (and total) time: about 25 minutes

Calories **185**
Protein **2g.**
Cholesterol **0mg.**
Total fat **1g.**
Saturated fat **0g.**
Sodium **23mg.**

| |
|---|
| 1 cup apple cider or unsweetened apple juice |
| 2 tbsp. mango chutney, coarsely chopped |
| 1 tsp. curry powder |
| 3 dried apricots, thinly sliced |
| 2 apples, preferably Granny Smith, cored and cut into 1-inch pieces |
| ¼ cup dark raisins |
| ¼ cup golden raisins |
| 1 medium cantaloupe, seeded and peeled, the flesh cut into 1-inch pieces |
| 1 large banana, peeled and cut into ¾-inch pieces |
| ½ tbsp. cornstarch, mixed with 1 tbsp. water |

Combine the cider or apple juice, chutney and curry powder in a large saucepan and bring the mixture to a boil. Reduce the heat to medium and simmer the mixture, partially covered, for five minutes. Add the apricots, apples, dark raisins and golden raisins and simmer them, covered, until the apples begin to soften — about three minutes.

Stir in the cantaloupe, the banana and the cornstarch mixture and simmer them, stirring occasionally, until the liquid has thickened — about two minutes. Serve the compote warm.

## Orange Slices
## with Pomegranate Seeds

Serves 6
Working time: about 15 minutes
Total time: about 45 minutes (includes chilling)

Calories **73**
Protein **1g.**
Cholesterol **0mg.**
Total fat **1g.**
Saturated fat **0g.**
Sodium **3mg.**

| |
|---|
| *3 navel oranges* |
| *1½ tbsp. finely chopped crystallized ginger* |
| *½ cup fresh orange juice* |
| *1 tbsp. dark rum* |
| *2 tbsp. sugar* |
| *½ tsp. pure vanilla extract* |
| *¼ cup pomegranate seeds, or 1 kiwi fruit, peeled, quartered and thinly sliced* |

Using a sharp, stainless-steel knife, cut off both ends of one of the oranges. Stand the orange on end and cut away vertical strips of the peel and pith. Slice the or-ange into ¼-inch-thick rounds. Peel and slice the re-maining oranges the same way.

Sprinkle the ginger into the bottom of a 9-inch nonreactive pie plate. Arrange the orange slices in a spiral pattern, overlapping them slightly, and set the pie plate aside.

Combine the orange juice, rum and sugar in a small nonreactive saucepan over medium-high heat and boil the mixture for five minutes. Remove the pan from the heat and let the syrup cool slightly, then stir in the vanilla. Pour the syrup over the orange slices and chill the fruit thoroughly.

Invert a serving plate over the pie plate, quickly turn both over together, and lift away the pie plate. Sprinkle the orange slices with the pomegranate seeds, or scat-ter the kiwi fruit over the oranges, and serve at once.

# Sliced Apples on Toast

Serves 6
Working time: about 30 minutes
Total time: about 35 minutes

Calories **191**
Protein **3g.**
Cholesterol **10mg.**
Total fat **5g.**
Saturated fat **3g.**
Sodium **121mg.**

| |
| --- |
| 2 tbsp. unsalted butter |
| 5 apples, peeled, halved, cored and thinly sliced |
| 3 tbsp. fresh lemon juice |
| 3 tbsp. maple syrup |
| 6 slices whole-wheat bread, toasted |
| 1 tbsp. sugar |

Preheat the oven to 500° F.

Melt the butter in a large, nonstick skillet over medi-um heat. Add the apples, lemon juice and maple syrup and cook the mixture until the apples are soft — about five minutes.

Drain the cooking liquid from the apples into a bowl and set it aside. Allow the apples to cool slightly. Divide the apples equally among the toasts, overlapping the apple slices slightly. Sprinkle each apple toast with some of the sugar.

Bake the apple toasts until the apples are hot and the bread is very crisp — about five minutes. Drizzle some of the reserved juice over each of the apple toasts and serve them hot.

# Cardamom Muffins

Makes 12 muffins
Working time: about 15 minutes
Total time: about 40 minutes

Calories **196**
Protein **4g.**
Cholesterol **6mg.**
Total fat **6g.**
Saturated fat **2g.**
Sodium **146mg.**

| |
|---|
| ¼ cup walnuts (about 1 oz.) |
| 1½ cups unbleached all-purpose flour |
| ¾ cup sugar |
| ½ tsp. ground cinnamon |
| ½ tsp. baking powder |
| ¼ tsp. salt |
| 2 tbsp. unsalted butter, cut into pieces and chilled |
| 2 tbsp. unsalted margarine, preferably corn oil, cut into pieces and chilled |
| 1 tsp. ground cardamom or ground allspice |
| 1 cup whole-wheat flour |
| ½ tsp. baking soda |
| 1¼ cups buttermilk |
| 1 tsp. pure vanilla extract |

Preheat the oven to 375° F. Lightly oil a muffin pan.

In a small baking pan, toast the walnuts in the oven until they are fragrant and slightly darker — about 10 minutes. Set the toasted nuts aside to cool.

In a bowl, combine the all-purpose flour, sugar, cinnamon, baking powder and salt. Using a pastry blender or two knives, cut in the butter and margarine until the mixture resembles coarse meal. Transfer ¼ cup of the mixture to a food processor; add the cardamom and the toasted walnuts and process to fine crumbs; this will be used as a topping for the muffins. Set the topping aside.

Add the whole-wheat flour and the baking soda to the remaining flour mixture and mix them in well. Pour in the buttermilk and vanilla, and stir the ingredients just until they are blended; do not overmix.

Spoon the batter into the muffin cups, filling each one about half full. Sprinkle the muffins with the crumb topping. Bake the muffins until they are well browned and firm to the touch — 20 to 25 minutes.

# Irish Soda Biscuits with Currants and Caraway Seeds

Makes 24 biscuits
Working time: about 15 minutes
Total time: about 30 minutes

Calories **86**
Protein **2g.**
Cholesterol **13mg.**
Total fat **2g.**
Saturated fat **1g.**
Sodium **118mg.**

| |
|---|
| 2 cups unbleached all-purpose flour |
| 1 cup whole-wheat flour |
| 2 tbsp. sugar |
| 2 tsp. baking powder |
| 1 tsp. baking soda |
| ¼ tsp. salt |
| 2 tbsp. cold unsalted margarine, preferably corn oil |
| 1 tbsp. cold unsalted butter |
| 1 tbsp. caraway seeds |
| 1 egg |
| 1 cup buttermilk |
| ½ cup currants |
| 2 tbsp. low-fat milk |

Preheat the oven to 350° F. In a bowl, combine the two flours, the sugar, baking powder, baking soda and salt. Using a pastry blender or two knives, cut in the margarine and butter until the mixture resembles coarse meal. In another bowl, whisk the caraway seeds, egg and buttermilk together. Stir the buttermilk mixture and the currants into the flour mixture. (The dough will become too stiff to stir before all the flour is mixed in.)

Turn the dough out onto a lightly floured surface and knead it gently just until all the flour is incorporated. Roll or pat out the dough so that it is about ¾ inch thick. Cut out rounds with a 2-inch biscuit cutter or the rim of a small glass, and place the biscuits on an ungreased baking sheet. Gather up the scraps of dough, form them into a ball, and repeat the process. Brush the biscuits with the milk and cut a cross on the top of each with the tip of a sharp knife or a pair of scissors. Bake the biscuits until they are golden brown — about 15 minutes. Serve the biscuits while they are hot.

# Spicy Corn Sticks

Makes 18 corn sticks
Working time: about 15 minutes
Total time: about 30 minutes

Calories **94**
Protein **3g.**
Cholesterol **16mg.**
Total fat **2g.**
Saturated fat **0g.**
Sodium **85mg.**

| |
|---|
| 1¼ cups unbleached all-purpose flour |
| 1 cup cornmeal |
| 2 tbsp. sugar |
| ¼ tsp. cayenne pepper |
| 1 tbsp. baking powder |
| 1 cup low-fat milk |
| 1 egg |
| 2 tbsp. safflower oil |
| ⅓ cup diced sweet red pepper |
| ⅓ cup diced green pepper |
| ½ cup fresh or frozen corn kernels |

Preheat the oven to 450° F. Lightly oil a corn-stick pan and heat it in the oven for 10 minutes.

Put the flour, cornmeal, sugar, cayenne pepper and baking powder into a bowl and mix them together. In another bowl, whisk together the milk, egg and oil. Pour the milk mixture into the dry ingredients and stir them just until they are blended. Stir in the red and green peppers and the corn.

Spoon the batter into the hot corn-stick pan, filling each mold about three-fourths full. Reduce the oven temperature to 400° F. and bake the corn sticks until a wooden pick inserted into the center comes out clean — 10 to 12 minutes. Keep the corn sticks warm while you bake the remaining batter. Five minutes before the last corn sticks are through baking, return the other corn sticks to the oven to reheat them. Serve the corn sticks at once.

EDITOR'S NOTE: *If a corn-stick pan is not available, the batter can be baked in a 10-inch cast-iron skillet instead. Increase the baking time to about 25 minutes; cut the cornbread into wedges to serve.*

## Our Basic Bagels

Makes 12 bagels
Working time: about 1 hour
Total time: about 1 hour and 30 minutes

Calories **137**
Protein **5g.**
Cholesterol **0mg.**
Total fat **1g.**
Saturated fat **0g.**
Sodium **95mg.**

| |
|---|
| 2 packages fast-rising dry yeast (about 2 tbsp.) |
| 4 tbsp. sugar |
| ½ tsp. salt |
| 2 cups unbleached all-purpose flour |
| 1½ cups whole-wheat flour |
| ¼ cup cornmeal |
| 1 egg white, beaten with 2 tbsp. water |
| 2 tbsp. caraway seeds, sesame seeds or poppy seeds, or ½ small onion, finely chopped (optional) |

In a large bowl, stir together the yeast, 2 tablespoons of the sugar, the salt, the all-purpose flour and ½ cup of the whole-wheat flour. In a small saucepan, heat 1½ cups of water just until it is hot to the touch (130° F.). Pour the water into the yeast-flour mixture and mix the dough thoroughly with a wooden spoon; the dough will be very soft. Gradually stir in enough of the remaining whole-wheat flour to form a stiff dough.

Turn the dough out onto a floured surface and knead it until it is smooth and elastic — about five minutes. Transfer the dough to a lightly oiled large bowl and turn the dough over to coat it with the oil. Cover the bowl with a damp towel or plastic wrap and place it in a warm, draft-free place. Let the dough rise until it has doubled in bulk — 15 to 20 minutes.

Meanwhile, pour 3 quarts of water into a large pot, add the remaining 2 tablespoons of sugar and heat the water until it is simmering. Preheat the oven to 450° F. Lightly butter a baking sheet and then sprinkle it with the cornmeal; set the baking sheet aside. If you plan to top the bagels with the chopped onion, lightly oil a small, nonstick skillet and sauté the onion until it is lightly browned.

Transfer the risen dough to a floured surface. Punch the dough down and then divide it into 12 pieces. Form each piece into a neat ball, rolling it around between the palms of your hands until it is smooth *(technique, below)*. To form rings, poke a floured finger through the center of each ball and move your finger in a circle to widen the hole until it is about 2 inches in diameter. Place the bagels on the work surface, cover them with a towel or plastic wrap, and let them rise until they are slightly larger — about five minutes.

With a slotted spoon, carefully put three or four bagels into the simmering water. Poach them for 30 seconds, turn them over, and poach them for 30 seconds more. Lift out the bagels and set them on a kitchen towel to drain. Repeat the process with the remaining bagels. When all of the bagels have been poached and drained, transfer them to the prepared baking sheet. Brush the bagels with the beaten egg white and, if you like, sprinkle them with some of the caraway, sesame or poppy seeds, or the sautéed onion.

Bake the bagels until they are well browned — about 25 minutes. Transfer the bagels to a rack to cool. If you like, serve the bagels with the Savory Vegetable Spread and the Smoked Salmon Spread *(box, page 51)*.

# Variations

## Rye Bagels

Substitute 2½ to 2¾ cups of unbleached all-purpose flour and 1 cup of rye flour for the flours in the basic recipe.

Combine the yeast, 2 tablespoons of the sugar, the salt, the rye flour and 1½ cups of the all-purpose flour in a large bowl. Pour in the hot water, as described, and mix the dough thoroughly. Add enough of the remaining all-purpose flour to form a stiff dough, then proceed with the basic bagel recipe.

## Whole-Wheat-and-Oat-Bran Bagels

Substitute 3 cups of unbleached all-purpose flour, ¾ cup of oat bran and ¼ to ½ cup of whole-wheat flour for the flours in the basic recipe.

Combine the yeast, 2 tablespoons of the sugar, the salt, 2 cups of the all-purpose flour and the oat bran in a large bowl. Pour in the hot water, as described, and mix the dough thoroughly. Add the remaining 1 cup of all-purpose flour and enough of the whole-wheat flour to make a stiff dough, then proceed with the basic bagel recipe.

## Making Bagels

**1** FORMING A BALL. After dividing the dough into 12 pieces (recipe, above), take a piece and roll it between your palms until it is smooth and spherical. Roll the other 11 pieces in the same manner.

**2** MAKING THE HOLE. Lightly flour a finger and press it into the center of a dough ball. Press hard enough to puncture the dough and touch the work surface beneath.

**3** ENLARGING THE OPENING. Place the index fingers of both hands through the hole, and gently rotate your fingers in a spinning motion to enlarge the opening until it is about 2 inches in diameter. Set the bagel aside and proceed to form and shape other dough balls.

# Pear Pizza

Serves 8
Working time: about 45 minutes
Total time: about 1 hour and 45 minutes

Calories **212**
Protein **4g.**
Cholesterol **4mg.**
Total fat **2g.**
Saturated fat **1g.**
Sodium **35mg.**

| |
|---|
| 1¾ cup bread flour |
| ½ cup sugar |
| 1 tsp. grated lemon zest |
| ⅛ tsp. salt |
| 1 package fast-rising dry yeast (about 1 tbsp.) |
| 1 tbsp. unsalted butter |
| ⅓ cup currants or raisins, coarsely chopped |
| 3 pears (about 1 ¼ lb.), quartered, cored, peeled and thinly sliced |
| 2 tbsp. fresh lemon juice |
| 2 tbsp. cornmeal |

In a large bowl, combine ½ cup of the flour, 2 tablespoons of the sugar, the lemon zest, salt and yeast. In a small saucepan, heat ¾ cup of water just until it is hot to the touch (130° F.), then pour it into the yeast-flour mixture, and mix the dough thoroughly with a wooden spoon. Gradually stir in enough of the remaining flour to make a dough that can be formed into a ball.

Transfer the dough to a floured surface and knead it until it is smooth and elastic — five to 10 minutes. Put the dough into a large, lightly oiled bowl and turn the dough over to coat it with the oil. Cover the bowl with a damp towel or plastic wrap. Place the bowl in a warm, draft-free place and let the dough rise until it has doubled in bulk — 30 to 45 minutes.

In the meantime, heat the butter in a large, heavy-bottomed skillet over medium-high heat. Add the currants or raisins and the pears, and cook the fruit, stirring frequently, for five minutes. Add the lemon juice and all but 1 tablespoon of the remaining sugar; continue cooking the mixture until the pears are soft and the sugar begins to brown — about five minutes more.

Preheat the oven to 450° F. Lightly oil a baking sheet and sprinkle it with the cornmeal. When the dough has risen, return it to the floured surface and knead it again for one minute. Flatten the dough into a 10-inch disk and transfer it to the baking sheet.

Spread the pear topping over the dough, leaving a ½-inch border of dough all around. Sprinkle the reserved tablespoon of sugar over the pear topping, then bake the pizza until the crust is well browned — about 20 minutes. Remove the pizza from the oven and let it stand for about five minutes before slicing it into wedges and serving it.

---

EDITOR'S NOTE: *This pizza can be stored for up to one day, wrapped in aluminum foil, and then reheated, unwrapped, in a 400° F. oven for 10 minutes.*

# Applesauce-and-Prune Bread

Serves 12
Working time: about 45 minutes
Total time: about 2 hours and 30 minutes
(includes cooling)

Calories **271**
Protein **3g.**
Cholesterol **0mg.**
Total fat **6g.**
Saturated fat **1g.**
Sodium **184mg.**

| |
|---|
| ¾ cup pitted prunes, halved |
| 6 large McIntosh apples, or other sweet, tangy cooking apples, peeled, quartered and cored |
| 2 cups unbleached all-purpose flour |
| ½ cup plus 1 tbsp. oat bran |
| 1 tbsp. unsweetened cocoa powder |
| 2 tsp. baking soda |
| ¼ tsp. salt |
| 1 tsp. ground cinnamon |
| ½ tsp. grated nutmeg |
| ¼ tsp. ground cloves |
| ½ cup plus 1 tbsp. sugar |
| ½ cup honey |
| ¼ cup safflower oil |

Put the prunes into a small bowl, pour 1 cup of boiling water over them, and set the bowl aside.

Put the apples into a large, heavy-bottomed saucepan and simmer them over low heat, stirring occasionally, until nearly all of the liquid has evaporated and the

apples have cooked down to a smooth, thick paste — about 30 minutes. Set the applesauce aside.

While the apples are simmering, mix the flour, ½ cup of the oat bran, the cocoa powder, baking soda, salt, cinnamon, ¼ teaspoon of the nutmeg and the cloves in a large bowl. In another bowl, combine ½ cup of the sugar, the honey and the oil.

Preheat the oven to 350° F. Lightly oil a 9-by-5-inch loaf pan.

Stir the applesauce into the sugar-honey mixture; add the sweetened applesauce to the flour mixture and stir well to make a smooth batter. Drain the prunes well, fold them into the batter, and spoon the batter into the prepared pan.

In a small bowl, mix the remaining 1 tablespoon of oat bran, the remaining 1 tablespoon of sugar and the remaining ¼ teaspoon of nutmeg; sprinkle this topping over the batter.

Bake the bread until a cake tester inserted into its center comes out clean — one hour to one hour and 10 minutes. Remove the bread from the oven and let it stand for five minutes. Run a knife blade around the sides of the pan, then invert the pan onto a cake rack, and rap it sharply to unmold the bread. Let the bread stand for 30 minutes before slicing and serving it.

# Cheese Pinwheels

Makes 8 pastries
Working time: about 30 minutes
Total time: about 45 minutes

*Per pinwheel:*
Calories **212**
Protein **7g.**
Cholesterol **2mg.**
Total fat **4g.**
Saturated fat **1g.**
Sodium **271mg.**

| |
|---|
| 1½ cups unbleached all-purpose flour |
| ¾ cup whole-wheat flour |
| 3 tbsp. granulated sugar |
| 2 tsp. baking powder |
| ½ tsp. baking soda |
| ⅛ tsp. salt |
| ¼ tsp. ground mace or ground cinnamon |
| 1 cup low-fat yogurt |
| 2 tbsp. safflower oil |
| ¼ cup confectioners' sugar, sifted |
| 2 tsp. low-fat milk |
| **Cheese-and-lemon filling** |
| ½ cup low-fat cottage cheese |
| 2 tsp. granulated sugar |
| grated zest of 1 lemon |

To make the filling, purée the cottage cheese in a food processor until no trace of curd remains. Add the 2 teaspoons of granulated sugar and the lemon zest; process the mixture until the ingredients are blended. (Alternatively, press the cheese through a fine sieve, add the sugar and the lemon zest, and stir well.) Set the filling aside.

Preheat the oven to 400° F.; lightly oil a baking sheet. Combine the flours, the 3 tablespoons of granulated sugar, the baking powder, baking soda, salt, and mace or cinnamon in a large bowl. In a smaller bowl, whisk together the yogurt and the oil; stir this mixture into the dry ingredients with a wooden spoon. Turn the dough onto a floured surface and knead it once or twice to fully incorporate the ingredients and make a soft dough.

Divide the dough in half. Roll one half of the dough into an 8-inch square, then cut the square into four 4-inch squares. Form a pinwheel, using 1 tablespoon of the cheese filling *(technique, right)*. With a spatula,

transfer the pinwheel to the baking sheet. Repeat the procedure with the remaining dough.

Bake the pinwheels until they are golden brown — 10 to 12 minutes. Just before the pastries are done, mix the confectioners' sugar and the milk in a small bowl. Drizzle or brush the sugar glaze over the pinwheels as soon as they are removed from the oven. Serve the pinwheels hot.

## Forming Pinwheels

1 SQUARING THE DOUGH. Onto a lightly floured work surface, roll out half of the dough into a sheet about 9 by 9 inches. With a sharp, small knife, trim the edges to straighten them, then divide the square into quarters (as shown). Discard the trimmings.

2 CUTTING CORNERS. Working with one dough square at a time, use the knife tip to slit each corner diagonally to within an inch of the center.

3 FILLING THE SQUARE. Place a heaping spoonful of the prepared cottage-cheese filling ( recipe, left) onto the center of the dough square.

4 FORMING THE PINWHEEL. With your fingers, lift and fold every other point over the filling. Press the last point down upon the others to keep them in place. Repeat the procedures to make the other pinwheels.

# Fruit-Filled Gems

GEMS ARE MINIATURE MUFFINS; GEM PANS ARE AVAILABLE AT
GOURMET AND PROFESSIONAL KITCHEN EQUIPMENT STORES.

Makes 24 gems
Working time: about 45 minutes
Total time: about 1 hour and 15 minutes

Per gem:
Calories **83**
Protein **1g.**
Cholesterol **14mg.**
Total fat **3g.**
Saturated fat **1g.**
Sodium **29mg.**

| |
| --- |
| 1 tart cooking apple, peeled, cored and coarsely grated |
| ½ cup chopped dried apricots |
| ½ cup apple cider or unsweetened apple juice |
| grated zest and juice of 1 lemon |
| ¾ cup sugar |
| 1¼ cup unbleached all-purpose flour |
| ¼ tsp. baking powder |
| 2 tbsp. unsalted butter |
| 2 tbsp. unsalted margarine, preferably corn oil |
| 1 egg, beaten |
| 2 tbsp. chopped almonds, toasted |

Combine the apple, apricots, cider or apple juice, lemon zest and juice, and ¼ cup of the sugar in a nonreactive saucepan and bring the mixture to a boil. Reduce the heat and simmer the mixture until the fruit is soft and most of the juice has evaporated — about 15 minutes. Set the filling aside and let it cool.

Combine the remaining sugar with the flour and baking powder in a bowl. Cut the butter and marga-rine into the dry ingredients with a pastry blender or two knives until the mixture resembles coarse meal. With your fingertips, work the egg into the dough just until the egg is incorporated and the dough begins to hold together. Shape two thirds of the dough into a log about 1 inch wide, wrap it in plastic wrap and chill it for 15 minutes. Shape the remaining dough into a round about ½ inch thick; wrap and chill it also.

Preheat the oven to 350° F.

Cut the dough log into 24 pieces and flatten each one slightly. Press one of the pieces into one of the cups of a gem pan to line it, molding the dough along the sides to the top of the cup. Use the remaining pieces of dough to make 23 more cups. Be careful not to leave any holes in the pastry or the gems will stick to the pan after they are baked. Spoon the fruit filling into the lined cups and sprinkle some of the almonds into each one of them.

Roll out the remaining dough on a lightly floured surface until it is about ⅛ inch thick and cut 24 rounds the same size as the tops of the gem cups. Cover each fruit gem with a round of pastry, lightly pressing on the edges of the pastry to seal them.

Bake the fruit gems until they are browned — 25 to 30 minutes. Let them cool slightly. To remove the gems, cover the pan with a baking sheet or a wire rack, turn both over together, and lift off the pan. Serve the fruit gems warm or at room temperature.

# Scallion and Rice Muffins

Makes 12 muffins
Working time: 20 minutes
Total time: 45 minutes

Per muffin:
Calories **106**
Protein **3g.**
Cholesterol **24mg.**
Total fat **3g.**
Saturated fat **1g.**
Sodium **131mg.**

| |
| --- |
| ¼ cup rice |
| 1 ½ cups unbleached all-purpose flour |
| 2 tsp. baking powder |
| 2 tsp. sugar |
| ¼ tsp. salt |
| ¼ tsp. ground white pepper |
| 1 egg |
| ¾ cup low-fat milk |
| 2 tbsp. safflower oil |
| 2 scallions, trimmed and finely chopped (about ¼ cup) |

Preheat the oven to 425° F. Lightly oil a muffin pan.

Bring ⅔ cup of water to a boil in a saucepan. Stir in the rice, then reduce the heat to low, and cover the pan tightly. Cook the rice until it is tender and all of the liquid has been absorbed — 15 to 20 minutes. Uncover the pan and set the rice aside to cool.

Sift the flour, baking powder, sugar, salt and pepper into a bowl. In another bowl, lightly beat the egg, then whisk in the milk and oil; stir in the cooled rice and the scallions. Pour the rice mixture into the flour mixture, then stir the ingredients just until they are blended.

Spoon the batter into the muffin cups, filling each one no more than two-thirds full. Bake the muffins until they are lightly browned — 18 to 22 minutes. Remove the muffins from the cups immediately and serve them hot.

## Spiced Sweet Potato Quick Bread

Serves 12
Working time: about 20 minutes
Total time: about 2 hours and 20 minutes
(includes cooling)

Calories **155**
Protein **3g.**
Cholesterol **24mg.**
Total fat **5g.**
Saturated fat **1g.**
Sodium **86mg.**

| |
|---|
| 1 cup unbleached all-purpose flour |
| ½ cup whole-wheat flour |
| 1 tsp. baking powder |
| ½ tsp. baking soda |
| 1 tsp. ground cinnamon |
| ½ tsp. ground allspice |
| 1 egg |
| ½ cup light or dark brown sugar |
| ¼ cup safflower oil |
| ½ cup low-fat milk |
| 1 cup peeled, grated, firmly packed sweet potato (about 6 oz.) |
| ½ cup currants or raisins (optional) |

Preheat the oven to 350° F. Lightly oil an 8-by-4-inch loaf pan.

Sift the two flours, baking powder, baking soda, cinnamon and allspice into a bowl; set the bowl aside. Put the egg and the sugar into a large bowl and beat the mixture until it is light and fluffy. Gradually add the oil and the milk and continue beating for one minute. Stir in the grated sweet potato and the currants or raisins, if you are using them. Add the sifted flour mixture, ½ cup at a time, mixing the batter after each addition just until the flour is blended. Spoon the batter into the pan.

Bake the loaf until it has shrunk from the sides of the pan and a cake tester inserted into the center comes out clean — 55 to 60 minutes. Let the bread stand for 10 minutes before turning it out onto a rack. Cool the bread completely before slicing it.

# Ricotta Muffins with Poppy Seeds

Makes 10 muffins
Working time: about 15 minutes
Total time: about 30 minutes

Per muffin:
Calories **212**
Protein **7g.**
Cholesterol **9mg.**
Total fat **7g.**
Saturated fat **2g.**
Sodium **188mg.**

| |
|---|
| 2 cups unbleached all-purpose flour |
| ½ cup sugar |
| 1 tsp. baking soda |
| ¼ tsp. salt |
| ¼ cup poppy seeds |
| 1 cup part-skim ricotta cheese |
| 2 tbsp. safflower oil |
| grated zest of 1 lemon |
| 1 tbsp. fresh lemon juice |
| ¾ cup low-fat milk |
| 2 egg whites |

Preheat the oven to 400° F. Lightly oil a muffin pan.

Sift the flour, sugar, baking soda and salt into a bowl; stir in the poppy seeds. In another bowl, combine the ricotta, oil, lemon zest and lemon juice, and then whisk in the milk. Add the ricotta mixture to the flour mixture and stir them just until they are blended; do not overmix.

Beat the egg whites until they form soft peaks. Stir half of the beaten egg whites into the batter, then fold in the remaining egg whites. Spoon the batter into the prepared muffin pan, filling each cup no more than two-thirds full, and bake the muffins until they are lightly browned — 12 to 14 minutes. Serve the muffins immediately.

# Filled Whole-Wheat Monkey Bread

THIS IS A REDUCED-FAT VERSION OF MONKEY BREAD, BALLS OF SWEET YEAST DOUGH BAKED IN A TUBE PAN.

Serves 8
Working time: about 30 minutes
Total time: about 2½ hours (includes rising)

Calories **352**
Protein **7g.**
Cholesterol **10mg.**
Total fat **7g.**
Saturated fat **3g.**
Sodium **157mg.**

| |
| --- |
| 2 cups unbleached all-purpose flour |
| 1 cup whole-wheat flour |
| ½ cup plus 1 tbsp. granulated sugar |
| ½ tsp. salt |
| 1 package fast-rising dry yeast (about 1 tbsp.) |
| 1 cup low-fat milk |
| ¼ cup dark raisins |
| ¼ cup golden raisins or chopped dried apricots |

| |
| --- |
| ¼ cup chopped walnuts |
| 1 tsp. unsweetened cocoa powder |
| ¼ cup dark brown sugar |
| 2 tbsp. honey |
| 1½ tsp. ground cinnamon |
| 2 tbsp. unsalted butter, melted |

To make the bread dough, mix the all-purpose flour, the whole-wheat flour, 1 tablespoon of the granulated sugar, the salt and the yeast together in a large bowl and make a well in the center of the dry ingredients. In a small saucepan, heat the milk just until it is hot to the touch (130° F.). Stir the hot liquid into the flour mixture.

Turn the dough out onto a floured surface and knead the dough until it is smooth and elastic — about 10 minutes. Put it into a large bowl, cover the bowl, and let the dough rise in a warm place until it has doubled in bulk — about 45 minutes.

For the filling, combine the dark raisins, golden raisins or apricots, walnuts, cocoa powder, brown sugar, honey and ½ teaspoon of the cinnamon in a bowl. In another bowl, combine the remaining ½ cup of granulated sugar and the remaining 1 teaspoon of cinnamon. Set the bowls aside.

Punch the dough down and turn it out onto a lightly floured surface. Form the dough into a log shape and cut the dough into 16 pieces. Flatten the pieces into 4-inch rounds.

Put about 2 tablespoons of the filling in the middle of each dough round and form a ball (technique, below). Lightly dip the ball into the melted butter, then roll it in the cinnamon-sugar mixture. Repeat this process with the remaining dough rounds and filling. Arrange the balls in a nonstick or lightly oiled 8-cup Bundt or tube pan with the pinched edges of the balls toward the inside. Cover the pan and let the dough rise until it has again doubled in bulk — about 30 minutes.

Preheat the oven to 375° F.

Bake the bread until it is browned and sounds hollow when tapped — 35 to 45 minutes. Put a serving plate on top of the pan and turn both over to invert the bread onto the plate. Serve the monkey bread warm.

## Preparing Monkey Bread

1 FILLING AND FORMING A BALL. After placing about 2 tablespoons of filling onto the middle of a dough round (recipe, left), gather up the sides of the round with your fingers. Pinch the rim together firmly to seal the filling inside.

2 COATING THE BALL. Dip the ball into the small container of melted butter. Then roll the ball in the prepared cinnamon-sugar mixture until it is completely coated.

3 ARRANGING THE BREAD. Put the ball into a nonstick or lightly oiled 8-cup Bundt or tube pan, with the pinched edge facing the hole of the pan. Fill, form and place the other balls in the same manner, packing them into the pan side by side. Cover the pan and bake as directed in the recipe.

# Potato-Basil Biscuits

Makes 16 biscuits
Working time: about 20 minutes
Total time: about 35 minutes

*Per biscuit:*
Calories **90**
Protein **2g.**
Cholesterol **1mg.**
Total fat **4g.**
Saturated fat **1g.**
Sodium **161mg.**

| |
|---|
| *1 medium russet or other baking potato (about ½ lb.), peeled and cut into 8 pieces* |
| *1½ cups unbleached all-purpose flour* |
| *1 tbsp. baking powder* |
| *¼ tsp. salt* |
| *1 tsp. sugar* |
| *¼ tsp. ground white pepper or freshly ground black pepper* |
| *5 tbsp. unsalted margarine, preferably corn oil, cut into small pieces and chilled* |
| *2 tbsp. chopped fresh basil, or 2 tsp. dried basil* |
| *½ cup low-fat milk* |

Preheat the oven to 425° F. Put the potato pieces into a saucepan and add enough water to cover them. Bring the water to a boil, then reduce the heat, and simmer the pieces until they are soft — 10 to 15 minutes.

While the potato is cooking, sift the flour, baking powder, salt, sugar and pepper into a bowl. Using two knives or a pastry blender, cut the margarine into the flour mixture until it resembles coarse meal. Stir in the basil, then set the flour mixture aside.

Drain the potato pieces, then transfer them to a bowl. Mash the potato with a potato masher or a fork; alternatively, work the potato through a food mill. Add the milk, then stir the mixture until it is well blended.

Add the flour mixture to the mashed potato. Stir the mixture with a wooden spoon to form a soft dough that does not stick to the sides of the bowl. If the mixture seems too dry, stir in additional milk, ½ teaspoon at a time.

Turn the dough out onto a floured surface and knead it gently just until it is smooth and all the ingredients have been incorporated — about eight times. Roll or pat out the dough so that it is about ½ inch thick and cut out rounds with a 2-inch biscuit cutter or the rim of a small glass. Place the biscuits on an ungreased baking sheet and bake them until they have puffed slightly and are golden brown — about 15 minutes. Serve the biscuits immediately.

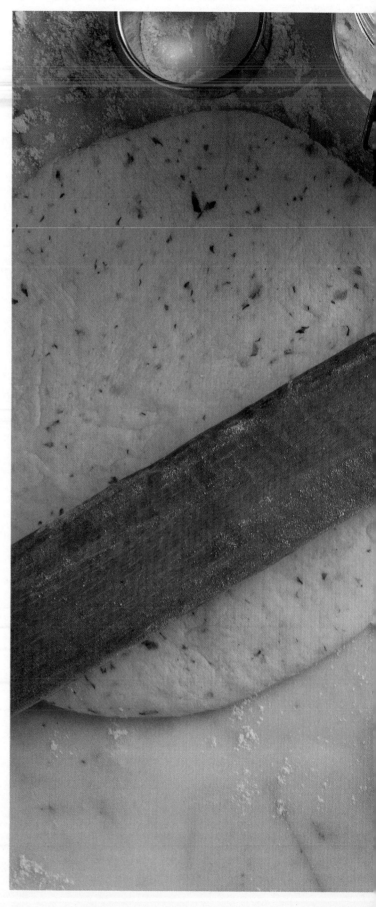

# Caramel-Orange-Pecan Sticky Buns

Serves 12
Working time: about 25 minutes
Total time: about 45 minutes

Calories **185**
Protein **3g.**
Cholesterol **1mg.**
Total fat **4g.**
Saturated fat **1g.**
Sodium **165mg.**

| |
|---|
| 2 tbsp. dark brown sugar |
| 1½ cups plus 1 tbsp. unbleached all-purpose flour |
| ½ tsp. ground cinnamon |
| ½ cup whole-wheat flour |
| 1 tbsp. granulated sugar |
| 1 tbsp. baking powder |
| ¼ tsp. salt |
| ¾ cup low-fat milk |
| 2 tbsp. safflower oil |
| grated zest of 1 orange |
| ¼ cup raisins |
| **Caramel-pecan topping** |
| ½ cup dark brown sugar |
| 2 tbsp. fresh orange juice |
| 2 tbsp. honey |
| ¼ cup chopped pecans (about 1 oz.) |

Preheat the oven to 375° F.

To make the caramel-pecan topping, combine the ½ cup brown sugar, the orange juice and the honey in a small saucepan. Bring the mixture to a boil, then reduce the heat and simmer the liquid for one minute. Stir in the pecans and then pour the topping into a 10-inch ring mold or an 8-inch-round cake pan.

Combine the 2 tablespoons of brown sugar, 1 tablespoon of the all-purpose flour and the cinnamon in a small bowl; set the bowl aside.

In a larger bowl, combine the remaining 1½ cups all-purpose flour, the whole-wheat flour, granulated sugar, baking powder and salt. Add the milk, oil and orange zest; stir the ingredients together just until they are blended; do not overmix. Turn the dough out onto a floured surface and gently knead it just until it is smooth. Roll the dough into an 8-by-12-inch oblong. Sprinkle the dough evenly with the reserved cinnamon mixture, then with the raisins.

Beginning with a long side, roll the dough into a log. Cut the log into 12 slices. Set the slices in the pan, on top of the pecan mixture. Bake the coffeecake until it is brown and the pecan mixture is bubbly — 20 to 25 minutes. Remove the pan from the oven and invert it immediately onto a large serving platter. Serve the coffeecake warm.

# Wheat Berry Muffins

Makes 12 muffins
Working time: about 20 minutes
Total time: about 45 minutes

*Per muffin:*
Calories **212**
Protein **7g.**
Cholesterol **47mg.**
Total fat **4g.**
Saturated fat **1g.**
Sodium **210mg.**

| |
|---|
| ½ cup wheat berries |
| 1¼ cups unbleached all-purpose flour |
| 1 cup whole-wheat flour |
| ½ cup nonfat dry milk |
| 1 tsp. baking powder |
| 1 tsp. baking soda |
| ½ tsp. ground cinnamon |
| ¼ tsp. salt |
| 2 eggs |
| ¼ cup honey |
| 2 tbsp. safflower oil |
| 1½ cups buttermilk |
| ½ cup raisins |

Bring 1 cup of water to a boil in a saucepan and then add the wheat berries. Reduce the heat to low, cover the pan, and simmer the kernels until they are tender — 15 to 20 minutes. If the wheat berries absorb all the water before they finish cooking, pour in more water, ¼ cup at a time, to keep the kernels from burning. Drain the wheat berries and set them aside.

Preheat the oven to 375° F. Lightly oil a muffin pan. Stir together the two flours, the dry milk, baking powder, baking soda, cinnamon and salt in a bowl. In another bowl, mix the eggs with the honey and the oil and then stir in the buttermilk. Combine the egg mixture with the flour mixture and stir them just until they are blended; do not overmix. Fold in the wheat berries and raisins.

Spoon the batter into the muffin cups, filling each one no more than two-thirds full. Bake the muffins until they are golden brown — 16 to 18 minutes. Serve the muffins immediately.

# Wheat Berry Bread

Makes 3 loaves
Working time: about 45 minutes
Total time: about 4 hours (includes rising)

*Per slice:*
Calories **105**
Protein **4g.**
Cholesterol **6mg.**
Total fat **1g.**
Saturated fat **0g.**
Sodium **38mg.**

| |
|---|
| 1 cup wheat berries |
| 1 envelope fast-rising dry yeast (about 1 tbsp.) |
| 2 tsp. sugar |
| ¼ cup nonfat dry milk |
| ¼ cup honey |
| ¼ cup molasses |
| ½ cup wheat germ |
| ¼ tsp. salt |
| 7 to 8 cups bread flour |
| 1 egg, beaten |
| ½ tsp. coarse salt |

Put the wheat berries and 3 cups of water into a saucepan and bring the water to a boil. Reduce the heat and simmer the wheat berries until they are tender — 30 to 45 minutes. Let the wheat berries cool in the cooking liquid, then drain them over a bowl; reserve the liquid.

Combine the yeast, sugar, dry milk, honey, molasses, wheat germ, salt and drained wheat berries with 6 cups of the flour in a large bowl. Measure the reserved cooking liquid and add enough water to make 3 cups of liquid. Heat the liquid just until it is hot to the touch (130° F.). Pour the hot liquid into the flour mixture and stir them together with a wooden spoon.

Gradually incorporate up to 2 cups of additional flour, working it in with your hands until the dough becomes stiff but not dry. Turn the dough out onto a floured surface and knead the dough until it is smooth and elastic — five to 10 minutes. Place the dough in a clean, oiled bowl; turn the dough over to coat it with the oil, cover the bowl with a damp towel or plastic wrap, and let the dough rise in a warm, draft-free place until it is doubled in size — about 45 minutes.

Punch the dough down and divide it into three pieces. Knead one piece of the dough and form it into a ball. Knead and form the remaining two pieces of dough into balls. Put the balls of dough onto a large baking sheet, leaving enough space between the loaves for them to expand. Cover the loaves and let them rise until they are doubled in volume again — about 30 minutes.

About 10 minutes before the end of the rising time, preheat the oven to 350° F.

Bake the loaves for 25 minutes. Remove the baking sheet from the oven, brush each loaf with some of the beaten egg, then sprinkle each with a little of the coarse salt. Return the loaves to the oven and continue to bake them until they are brown and sound hollow when tapped on the bottom — 25 to 30 minutes more. Let the loaves cool to room temperature; each yields 16 slices.

EDITOR'S NOTE: *If you plan to store the bread, it is preferable to keep it in the freezer. Refrigeration causes bread to dry out.*

## Pear Butter

Makes 1½ cups
Working time: about 25 minutes
Total time: about 2 hours and 30 minutes
(includes chilling)

Per tablespoon:
Calories **30**
Protein **0g.**
Cholesterol **0mg.**
Total fat **0g.**
Saturated fat **0g.**
Sodium **1mg.**

| |
|---|
| 2 lb. ripe pears, peeled, quartered, cored and cut into 1-inch pieces |
| 1 cup apple cider or unsweetened apple juice |
| 1 tbsp. light or dark brown sugar |
| ¼ tsp. ground allspice |
| ⅛ tsp. ground cinnamon |
| 1½ tbsp. pear liqueur or brandy |

Combine the pears, cider or apple juice, brown sugar, allspice and cinnamon in a large, heavy-bottomed saucepan. Bring the mixture to a simmer over medium heat, then reduce the heat to maintain a slow simmer. Cook the pears, stirring occasionally, until they are very soft and all the liquid has evaporated — about 1½ hours.

Put the pear mixture into a blender or a food processor, and add the liqueur or brandy. Process the mixture until the pears are smoothly puréed. Spoon the pear butter into a serving bowl and serve it at room temperature. Pear butter can be made up to a week in advance; cover it and store it in the refrigerator.

## Apricot Spread

Makes 1½ cups
Working time: about 10 minutes
Total time: about 25 minutes

Per tablespoon:
Calories **29**
Protein **0g.**
Cholesterol **0mg.**
Total fat **0g.**
Saturated fat **0g.**
Sodium **1mg.**

| |
|---|
| ½ lb. dried apricots |
| 1½ cups apple cider or unsweetened apple juice |
| ⅛ tsp. ground allspice |
| ½ tsp. ground cumin |

Put the apricots, cider or apple juice, allspice and cumin into a nonreactive saucepan. Bring the mixture to a simmer and cook it, stirring occasionally, until only about ½ cup of liquid remains — 10 to 15 minutes. Purée the mixture in a food processor for five seconds, then scrape down the sides, and process again to make a thick, chunky spread — about 10 seconds. The spread may be kept refrigerated for up to two weeks.

# Apple-Rhubarb Butter

Makes 4 cups
Working (and total) time: about 45 minutes

*Per tablespoon:*
Calories **12**
Protein **0g.**
Cholesterol **0mg.**
Total fat **0g.**
Saturated fat **0g.**
Sodium **0mg.**

| |
|---|
| *1 lb. fresh rhubarb, cut into 1-inch pieces, or* |
| *1 lb. frozen rhubarb, thawed* |
| *2 large McIntosh or other sweet, tangy apples* |
| *(about ¾ lb.), peeled, cored and sliced* |
| *grated zest and juice of 1 orange* |
| *½ cup sugar* |
| *¼ tsp. ground mace or grated nutmeg* |

Put the rhubarb, apples, orange zest, orange juice and sugar into a heavy-bottomed saucepan. Cook the mixture over medium-low heat, stirring occasionally with a wooden spoon to break up the pieces of fruit, until the mixture is very thick — 25 to 30 minutes. Stir in the mace or nutmeg, and serve the apple-rhubarb butter warm with pancakes or French toast, or chilled with muffins or biscuits.

# Fresh Yogurt Cheese

Makes 1½ cups
Working time: about 20 minutes
Total time: about 8 hours

*Per tablespoon:*
*Plain:*
Calories **18**
Protein **0g.**
Cholesterol **2mg.**
Total fat **0g.**
Saturated fat **0g.**
Sodium **10mg.**

*3 cups plain low-fat yogurt*

Line a large sieve with a double layer of cheesecloth or a large, round paper coffee filter. Place the lined sieve over a deep bowl so that the yogurt can effectively drain; spoon the yogurt into the sieve. Cover the bowl and sieve with plastic wrap. Put the bowl in the refrigerator and let the yogurt drain overnight.

Discard the whey that has collected in the bowl and transfer the yogurt cheese to another bowl; the cheese should be very thick. Cover the bowl with plastic wrap and refrigerate the cheese until you are ready to use it. Yogurt cheese will keep in the refrigerator for two weeks.

## Transforming Yogurt into Tangy Cheese Spreads

Yogurt plays an important role in a healthy, low-fat diet. In cooking, it provides a tasty alternative to sour cream and heavy cream. And with the simple cheese-making technique presented at left, yogurt can even take the place of cream cheese in your breakfast or brunch menu, especially when it is combined with other ingredients to yield savory spreads.

Yogurt cheese made from plain low-fat yogurt has all the delectability of cream cheese, but has 64 percent fewer calories and 90 percent less saturated fat. Its lighter texture (yogurt cheese contains no gum arabic, a thickener found in most commercial cream cheeses) and its tart, fresh flavor recommend it for morning meals and snacks. Furthermore, yogurt cheese is more easily digested than cream cheese and can be readily eaten by many who have lactose intolerance.

## Dill-and-Chive Spread

Makes 1½ cups
Working (and total) time: about 15 minutes

Per tablespoon:
Dill:
Calories **18**
Protein **2g.**
Cholesterol **2mg.**
Total fat **0g.**
Saturated fat **0g.**
Sodium **32mg.**

| |
|---|
| 1½ cups yogurt cheese (recipe, page 50) |
| 2 tbsp. finely cut fresh dill |
| 2 tbsp. finely cut fresh chives |
| ¼ tsp. salt |
| freshly ground black pepper |

Combine the yogurt cheese with the dill, chives, salt and a generous grinding of pepper. The spread may be served at once or covered and refrigerated until you are ready to use it.

## Savory Vegetable Spread

Makes 2 cups
Working time: about 30 minutes
Total time: about 2 hours and 30 minutes
(includes chilling)

Per tablespoon:
Veg:
Calories **15**
Protein **1g.**
Cholesterol **1mg.**
Total fat **0g.**
Saturated fat **0g.**
Sodium **42mg.**

| |
|---|
| 1 small carrot, finely shredded or grated (about ¼ cup) |
| 1 small sweet red pepper, seeded, deribbed and quartered, the flesh finely grated and the skin discarded |
| 3 radishes, finely grated |
| ½ small onion, finely grated |
| ½ tsp. salt |
| 2 garlic cloves, finely chopped |
| 2 tsp. fresh thyme, finely chopped, or ½ tsp. dried thyme leaves |
| 1½ cups yogurt cheese (recipe, page 50) |

Put the carrot and red pepper into a small, nonstick skillet, and cook them over low heat until most of their moisture has evaporated — three to four minutes. Let the vegetables cool.

Stir the cooled carrot and red pepper, along with the radishes, onion, salt, garlic and thyme, into the yogurt cheese. So that the flavors can meld, refrigerate the spread for at least two hours before serving it.

## Smoked Salmon Spread

Makes 1½ cups
Working time: about 15 minutes
Total time: about 2 hours and 15 minutes
(includes chilling)

Per tablespoon:
Salmon:
Calories **21**
Protein **2g.**
Cholesterol **3mg.**
Total fat **1g.**
Saturated fat **0g.**
Sodium **21mg.**

| |
|---|
| 1½ cups yogurt cheese (recipe, page 50) |
| 3 tbsp. finely cut fresh chives or scallions |
| 1½ oz. smoked salmon, very finely chopped |
| ¼ tsp. white pepper |
| ⅛ tsp. paprika, preferably Hungarian |
| 1 tsp. fresh lemon juice |
| ⅛ tsp. salt |

Combine the yogurt cheese with the chives, salmon, pepper, paprika, lemon juice and salt. So that the flavors can meld, refrigerate the spread for at least two hours before serving it.

## Sage and Black Pepper Waffles with Spiced Applesauce

Makes six 7-inch-round waffles
Working (and total) time: about 45 minutes

Calories **445**
Protein **10g.**
Cholesterol **47mg.**
Total fat **11g.**
Saturated fat **1g.**
Sodium **304mg.**

| |
| --- |
| 2 cups unbleached all-purpose flour |
| 2 tsp. baking powder |
| 2 tbsp. sugar |
| 2 tbsp. chopped fresh sage, or 2 tsp. ground sage |
| ½ cup cornmeal |
| ¼ tsp. salt |
| ¾ tsp. ground black pepper |
| 1 egg, separated, plus 2 egg whites |
| 2 cups skim milk |
| ¼ cup safflower oil |
| **Spiced applesauce** |
| 4 large McIntosh apples (about 1 ½ lb.), peeled, cored and cut into chunks |
| ¼ cup sugar |
| ¼ cup apple cider, unsweetened apple juice or water |
| ¼ tsp. grated nutmeg |

To make the spiced applesauce, first put the apples, the sugar and the cider, juice or water into a heavy-bottomed nonreactive saucepan. Bring the mixture to a boil. Reduce the heat and simmer the mixture, stirring occasionally, until the apples begin to lose their shape — 20 to 25 minutes. Remove the pan from the heat and stir in the nutmeg; the applesauce will be chunky. Cover the pan and set the applesauce aside while you make the waffles.

Sift the flour, baking powder and sugar into a bowl; stir in the sage, cornmeal, salt and pepper. In a second bowl, beat the egg yolk lightly and then whisk in the milk and oil. In another bowl, beat the egg whites until they form soft peaks. Make a well in the center of the flour mixture and pour in the milk mixture. Stir the batter just until it is blended; some lumps will remain. Stir about one fourth of the egg whites into the batter, then gently fold in the remaining whites.

Prepare the waffle iron according to the manufacturer's instructions. Ladle enough of the batter onto the preheated surface of the grid to cover it by about two thirds. Close the lid and bake the waffle until steam no longer escapes from the sides of the iron and the waffle is crisp and golden — three to five minutes. Serve the waffle immediately, topped with some of the applesauce; if the applesauce has cooled, reheat it beforehand. Continue making waffles in the same manner until no batter remains. Although these waffles are best served immediately, you may transfer them as you make them to an ovenproof plate and keep them in a 200° F. oven until all are ready.

EDITOR'S NOTE: *The spiced applesauce for this recipe can be prepared up to one day ahead, stored in the refrigerator, and heated just before serving.*

# Gingerbread Waffles

Serves 6
Working (and total) time: about 30 minutes

Calories **354**
Protein **11g.**
Cholesterol **50mg.**
Total fat **7g.**
Saturated fat **1g.**
Sodium **316mg.**

1 cup unbleached all-purpose flour
1 cup whole-wheat flour
½ cup sugar
1 tsp. ground cinnamon
1 tsp. ground ginger
1 tsp. dry mustard
½ tsp. baking soda
½ tsp. baking powder
¼ tsp. ground cloves
¼ tsp. salt
1¼ cups buttermilk
1 egg, separated, plus 1 egg white
¼ cup dark molasses
2 tbsp. safflower oil
julienned zest of 1 lemon, for garnish

**Lemon-yogurt topping**

1 cup plain low-fat yogurt
1 tbsp. fresh lemon juice
1 egg white
2 tbsp. sugar

To make the topping, combine the yogurt and lemon juice in a bowl. Beat the egg white with the sugar in a bowl until soft peaks form. Fold the beaten egg white into the yogurt mixture. Set the topping aside while you make the waffles.

Combine the flours, sugar, cinnamon, ginger, mustard, baking soda, baking powder, cloves and salt in a bowl. In another bowl, whisk together the buttermilk, egg yolk, molasses and oil; pour this mixture into the dry ingredients. Stir the batter until the ingredients are just blended; do not overmix.

Beat the 2 egg whites until they form soft peaks. Gently fold them into the batter. Prepare the waffle iron according to the manufacturer's instructions. Ladle enough of the batter onto the preheated surface of the grid to cover it by two thirds. Close the lid and bake the waffle until steam no longer escapes from the sides of the iron and the waffle is crisp and golden — three to five minutes. Continue making waffles in the same manner until all of the batter is used. Although these waffles are best served immediately, you may transfer them to an ovenproof plate as you make them, and keep them warm in a 200° F. oven until all are ready.

Garnish the waffles with some of the zest and serve them at once with the lemon-yogurt topping.

# Overnight French Toast

ALLOWING THE SOAKED BREAD SLICES TO REST OVERNIGHT
YIELDS SOFT AND CREAMY CENTERS.

Serves 6
Working time: about 30 minutes
Total time: about 8 hours and 30 minutes
(includes chilling)

Calories **298**
Protein **12g.**
Cholesterol **98mg.**
Total fat **4g.**
Saturated fat **2g.**
Sodium **529mg.**

| | |
|---|---|
| 1 loaf (about 1 lb.) unsliced French or Italian bread, the ends trimmed | |
| 2 eggs, plus 2 egg whites | |
| ⅓ cup sugar | |
| grated zest of 2 lemons | |
| ¼ tsp. salt | |
| 2 cups low-fat milk | |
| 2 tbsp. light or dark rum, or 1 tsp. pure vanilla extract | |
| freshly grated nutmeg | |

Cut the bread into 12 slices about ¾ inch thick. In a large, shallow dish, whisk together the eggs, egg whites, sugar, lemon zest and salt, then whisk in the milk and the rum or vanilla.

Dip the bread slices into the egg-and-milk mixture, turning them once or twice until they are thoroughly soaked with the liquid. Transfer the slices to a large plate as you work. Drizzle any liquid remaining in the dish over the slices, then sprinkle some nutmeg over them. Cover the slices with plastic wrap and refrigerate them overnight.

Preheat the oven to 400° F. Heat a large griddle or skillet (box, page 55) over medium heat until a few drops of cold water dance when sprinkled on the surface. Put as many prepared bread slices as will fit on the griddle or skillet and cook them until the undersides are golden — about three minutes. Turn the slices and cook them until the second sides are lightly browned — two to three minutes more. Transfer the slices to a baking sheet. Brown the remaining slices and transfer them to the baking sheet.

Place the baking sheet in the oven and bake the French toast until it is cooked through and has puffed up — about 10 minutes. Serve it hot with blueberry syrup (page 55) or another topping of your choice.

# Blueberry Syrup

Makes about 3½ cups
Working (and total) time: about 15 minutes

| | |
|---|---|
| *Per 3 tablespoons:* | *2 cups fresh blueberries, picked over and stemmed, or* |
| Calories **54** | *2 cups frozen whole blueberries* |
| Protein **0g.** | |
| Cholesterol **0mg.** | *1 cup sugar* |
| Total fat **0g.** | *1 lemon, the zest julienned and the juice reserved* |
| Saturated fat **0g.** | *1 navel orange, the zest julienned and the juice reserved* |
| Sodium **1mg.** | *1 tbsp. cornstarch, mixed with 1 tbsp. water* |

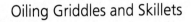

Combine 1 cup water, the blueberries, sugar, lemon zest and lemon juice, and orange zest and orange juice in a saucepan; bring the mixture to a boil. Reduce the heat to medium low and simmer the blueberries, stirring, for one minute.

Remove the saucepan from the heat and stir in the cornstarch mixture. Return the pan to the heat and simmer the syrup until it becomes thick and clear — about one minute more.

## Oiling Griddles and Skillets

While the higher fat content of traditional recipes allows you to cook on the well-seasoned surface of a griddle or skillet without using additional fat, the low-fat recipes in this book often require a slightly different approach to guard against sticking.

A nonstick griddle or skillet that has been maintained according to the manufacturer's instructions need not be oiled. However, if either is beginning to show signs of wear — particularly scratches — it is a good idea to coat the surface with a film of oil. Pour ¼ teaspoon of safflower oil onto the griddle or into the skillet and rub it all over the bottom with a paper towel. Do not discard the towel; it will have absorbed enough oil to allow you to coat the surface several times as needed during the cooking process.

A well-seasoned, heavy griddle or skillet that does not have a nonstick surface should be treated in the same way, but with 1 teaspoon of oil instead of ¼ teaspoon. In both cases, most of the oil will be retained by the towel and thus have little effect on the final calorie count.

## Whole-Wheat Yogurt Waffles with Fruit Salsa

Makes about six 7-inch-round waffles
Working (and total) time: about 30 minutes

Calories **393**
Protein **16g.**
Cholesterol **97mg.**
Total fat **11g.**
Saturated fat **2g.**
Sodium **396mg.**

| |
| --- |
| 1 cup unbleached all-purpose flour |
| 1 cup whole-wheat flour |
| 1 cup wheat germ |
| 1 tsp. baking powder |
| ½ tsp. baking soda |
| ½ tsp. salt |
| 2 eggs, separated |
| 2 tbsp. safflower oil |
| 3 tbsp. light or dark brown sugar |
| 1 cup low-fat milk |
| 1 cup plain low-fat yogurt |
| **Fruit salsa** |
| 2 cups fresh strawberries, hulled and quartered |
| 1 cup diced ripe papaya (or mango, peach, melon or pineapple) |
| 2 tbsp. honey |

To make the fruit salsa, combine the fruit with the honey and let the mixture stand at room temperature for 30 minutes.

Put the two flours, the wheat germ, baking powder, baking soda and salt into a bowl. In another bowl, lightly beat the egg yolks with the oil and brown sugar. Stir in the milk and yogurt. Pour the yogurt mixture into the flour mixture. Stir the ingredients together until they are just blended; do not overmix the batter.

Prepare the waffle iron according to the manufacturer's instructions. Beat the egg whites until they form soft peaks and then fold them into the batter. Ladle enough of the batter onto the preheated surface of the grid to cover it by about two thirds. Close the lid and bake the waffle until steam no longer escapes from the sides of the iron and the waffle is crisp and golden — three to five minutes. Serve the waffle at once, topped with the fruit salsa, and continue making waffles in the same manner until all of the batter is used. Although these waffles are best served immediately, you may transfer them as you make them to an ovenproof plate and keep them in a 200° F. oven until all are ready.

# Apple French Toast

Serves 6
Working (and total) time: about 30 minutes

Calories **314**
Protein **10g.**
Cholesterol **94mg.**
Total fat **5g.**
Saturated fat **2g.**
Sodium **454mg.**

| |
|---|
| 1 loaf (about 1 lb.) unsliced day-old dense white bread, the ends trimmed |
| 2 eggs, plus 2 egg whites |
| 2 tbsp. sugar |
| ¼ tsp. salt |
| 1 cup low-fat milk |
| ½ cup apple cider or unsweetened apple juice |
| 1 orange (optional), peeled and thinly sliced, the slices halved |

**Apple compote**

| |
|---|
| 1 apple, preferably Granny Smith, peeled, quartered, cored and chopped |
| 1 cup apple cider or unsweetened apple juice |
| ½ cup fresh orange juice |
| ⅓ cup sugar |
| 2 tbsp. currants |
| grated zest of 1 orange |
| ¼ tsp. grated nutmeg |
| pinch of salt |
| 1 tbsp. cornstarch, mixed with 1 tbsp. water |

Cut the bread into 12 slices about ½ inch thick; cut each slice into four strips. In a large, shallow dish, whisk together the eggs, egg whites, sugar and salt, then whisk in the milk and the cider or apple juice.

Dip the bread strips into the egg-and-milk mixture, turning them once or twice until they are thoroughly soaked with the liquid. Transfer the strips to a large plate or baking sheet as you work. Drizzle any liquid left in the dish over the strips.

To make the apple compote, combine the chopped apple, the cider or apple juice, orange juice, sugar, currants, orange zest, nutmeg and salt in a saucepan. Bring the liquid to a boil, reduce the heat to medium low, and simmer the compote until the apple is barely tender — about five minutes. Remove the pan from the heat and stir in the cornstarch mixture. Return the pan to the heat and simmer the compote, stirring, until it is thick and clear — about one minute. Transfer the compote to a serving bowl and keep it warm.

Heat a large griddle or skillet (box, page 55) over medium heat until a few drops of cold water dance when sprinkled on the surface. Cook the prepared strips of bread until the undersides are golden — about three minutes. Turn the strips over and cook them until the second sides are lightly browned — two to three minutes more. Transfer the French toast strips to a platter and keep them warm while you cook the remaining strips.

Serve the French toast at once, garnished with the orange slices, if you are using them, and accompanied by the apple compote.

## Spicy Shrimp Griddlecakes

Serves 6
Working (and total) time: about 30 minutes

Calories **246**
Protein **12g.**
Cholesterol **68mg.**
Total fat **6g.**
Saturated fat **3g.**
Sodium **294mg.**

| |
|---|
| 1¼ cups cornmeal |
| ½ cup unbleached all-purpose flour |
| 2 tsp. baking powder |
| 1 tsp. dried thyme leaves |
| 1 tsp. dried oregano |
| ¼ tsp. salt |
| ¼ tsp. ground white pepper |
| ¼ tsp. cayenne pepper |
| 3 large garlic cloves, finely chopped |
| 1 scallion, finely chopped |
| 1 small sweet red pepper, seeded, deribbed and finely chopped |
| 2 tbsp. unsalted butter, melted |
| 1 ⅔ cups low-fat milk |
| ½ lb. cooked, peeled baby shrimp |

| |
|---|
| 1 lemon, cut into wedges, for garnish |
| several parsley sprigs for garnish |

Combine the cornmeal, flour, baking powder, thyme, oregano, salt, white pepper and cayenne pepper in a bowl. Stir in the garlic, scallion and red pepper. Whisk in the melted butter and the milk, mixing until all the ingredients are just blended. Stir in the shrimp.

Heat a large griddle or skillet *(box, page 55)* over medium heat until a few drops of cold water dance when sprinkled on the surface. Drop the batter a generous tablespoon at a time onto the griddle and use the back of the spoon to spread the batter into rounds. Cook the griddlecakes until they are covered with bubbles and the undersides are golden — one to three minutes. Flip the griddlecakes and cook them until the second sides are lightly browned — about one minute more. Transfer the griddlecakes to a platter and keep them warm while you cook the remaining batter. Serve the griddlecakes piping hot, garnished with the lemon wedges and parsley sprigs.

# Tropical Puffed Pancake

Serves 4
Working time: about 30 minutes
Total time: about 45 minutes

Calories **349**
Protein **9g.**
Cholesterol **141mg.**
Total fat **8g.**
Saturated fat **2g.**
Sodium **265mg.**

| |
|---|
| 3 tbsp. granulated white sugar |
| ¼ tsp. ground cinnamon |
| ¼ cup unbleached all-purpose flour |
| ¼ cup whole-wheat flour |
| ½ tsp. baking powder |
| ¼ tsp. salt |
| 2 eggs, separated, plus 1 egg white |
| 1 tbsp. light or dark rum |
| 1 tbsp. safflower oil |
| grated zest of 1 lemon |
| ¾ cup low-fat milk |
| 2 bananas, sliced diagonally into ¼-inch-thick ovals |

**Rum-pineapple topping**

| |
|---|
| 1 pineapple, peeled, cored and coarsely chopped (about 2 cups), or 2 cups canned unsweetened pineapple chunks, drained and coarsely chopped |
| 2 tbsp. dark brown sugar |
| 2 tbsp. raisins |
| juice of 1 lemon |
| 2 tbsp. light or dark rum |

To make the rum-pineapple topping, put the pineapple into a heavy-bottomed saucepan, then stir in the brown sugar, raisins and lemon juice. Bring the mixture to a boil, then reduce the heat, and simmer the mixture for five minutes. Remove the pan from the heat and stir in the rum. Keep the topping warm while you prepare the puffed pancake.

In a small bowl, mix 2 tablespoons of the granulated white sugar with the cinnamon; set the cinnamon sugar aside. Preheat the oven to 425° F.

Sift the two flours, the baking powder, the salt and the remaining tablespoon of white sugar into a bowl. In a separate bowl, whisk the egg yolks with the rum and the oil; stir in the lemon zest and the milk. Whisk the flour mixture into the milk mixture to make a smooth, thin batter.

Beat the egg whites until they form soft peaks. Stir half of the egg whites into the batter and then fold in the remaining egg whites.

Heat a 12-inch ovenproof skillet over medium heat. Ladle the batter into the skillet. Cook the pancake for two minutes; top it with the sliced bananas and sprinkle it with the cinnamon sugar. Put the skillet into the oven and bake the pancake until it puffs up and is golden brown — 10 to 12 minutes. Slide the puffed pancake out of the pan onto a warmed serving plate. Cut the pancake into four wedges and serve it immediately with the rum-pineapple topping.

## Potato Pancakes with Apple-Mustard Compote

Serves 8
Working time: about 45 minutes
Total time: about 1 hour and 10 minutes

| | |
|---|---|
| Calories **204** | 1 medium russet or other baking potato (about ½ lb.), peeled and diced |
| Protein **3g.** | |
| Cholesterol **42mg.** | 1 egg, separated, plus 1 egg white |
| Total fat **4g.** | 1 tsp. sugar |
| Saturated fat **2g.** | ¼ tsp. salt |
| Sodium **162mg.** | ⅛ tsp. grated nutmeg |
| | ½ cup unbleached all-purpose flour |

**Apple-mustard compote**

| |
|---|
| 6 firm, tart apples that will hold their shape when cooked, preferably Granny Smith, quartered, cored, peeled and cut into eighths |
| ⅓ cup sugar |
| ⅓ cup apple cider or unsweetened apple juice |
| 2 tbsp. butter |
| ¼ cup golden raisins |
| grated zest and juice of 1 lemon |
| ½ tsp. ground cinnamon |
| 2 tbsp. grainy mustard |

Put the potato into a saucepan and cover it with water. Bring the water to a boil, then reduce the heat, and simmer the potato until it is soft — 10 to 15 minutes.

While the potato is cooking, prepare the apple-mustard compote. Put the apples, sugar, cider or apple juice, butter, raisins, lemon zest and lemon juice into a heavy-bottomed skillet over medium-high heat. Cook the mixture, stirring frequently, until the apples are heated through and tender — about five minutes. Stir in the cinnamon and mustard, and keep the compote warm while you make the pancakes. (If you like, you can make the compote a day ahead and reheat it.)

Drain the cooked potato, reserving 1 cup of the cooking liquid. Put the potato into a bowl and mash it with a potato masher or a fork until it is smooth; alternatively, work the potato through a food mill. Stir in the reserved cooking liquid and let the mashed potato cool to lukewarm.

Stir the egg yolk, sugar, salt and nutmeg into the mashed potatoes. Sift in the flour and stir the mixture just until it is blended.

Put the egg whites into a bowl and beat them until they form soft peaks. Stir about one fourth of the egg whites into the potato mixture and then gently fold in the remaining egg whites.

Heat a large griddle or skillet (box, page 55) over

medium heat until a few drops of cold water dance when sprinkled on the surface. Spoon about ¼ cup of the batter at a time onto the hot griddle or skillet and use the back of the spoon to spread the batter into rounds. Cook the pancakes until they are covered with bubbles and the undersides are golden — one to three minutes. Flip the pancakes and cook them until the second sides are lightly browned — about one minute more. Transfer the pancakes to a platter and keep them warm while you cook the remaining batter. Serve the pancakes immediately together with the apple-mustard compote.

# Cornmeal Buttermilk Pancakes

Serves 6
Working (and total) time: about 20 minutes

Calories **286**
Protein **8g.**
Cholesterol **94mg.**
Total fat **7g.**
Saturated fat **1g.**
Sodium **245mg.**

| |
|---|
| 1 ¼ cups unbleached all-purpose flour |
| 3 tbsp. sugar |
| ½ tsp. baking soda |
| ¼ tsp. salt |
| 1 cup cornmeal |
| 2 eggs |
| 1 ½ cups buttermilk |
| 2 tbsp. safflower oil |

Sift the flour, sugar, baking soda and salt into a bowl; stir in the cornmeal. In another bowl whisk together the eggs, buttermilk and oil.

Pour the buttermilk mixture into the dry ingredients and whisk them quickly together until they are just blended; do not overmix.

Heat a large griddle or skillet *(box, page 55)* over medium heat until a few drops of cold water dance when sprinkled on the surface. Drop 2 tablespoons of the batter onto the hot griddle or skillet, and use the back of the spoon to spread the batter into a round. Fill the skillet with pancakes; cook them until the tops are covered with bubbles and the undersides are golden — one or two minutes. Flip the pancakes over and cook them until the second sides are lightly browned — about one minute more. Transfer the pancakes to a platter and keep them warm while you cook the remaining batter.

Serve the pancakes immediately, accompanied by a topping of your choice.

# Orange French Toast

Serves 8
Working time: about 30 minutes
Total time: about 45 minutes

Calories **385**
Protein **10g.**
Cholesterol **103mg.**
Total fat **6g.**
Saturated fat **1g.**
Sodium **375mg.**

| |
| --- |
| ¼ cup sliced almonds |
| 1 loaf (about 1 lb.) unsliced day-old dense white or whole-wheat bread, the ends trimmed |
| 3 eggs, plus 3 egg whites |
| ¼ cup granulated white sugar |
| ¼ tsp. salt |
| grated zest of 1 orange |
| 1 tsp. pure vanilla extract |
| 1½ cups fresh orange juice |
| **Orange syrup** |
| 1 cup light brown sugar |
| 6 oz. frozen orange-juice concentrate |

Preheat the oven to 375° F. In a small, heavy-bottomed skillet set over medium heat, toast the sliced almonds, stirring constantly, until they are golden brown — about five minutes. Remove the almonds from the pan and set them aside.

Cut the bread into 16 slices about ½ inch thick. In a shallow dish, whisk together the eggs, egg whites, granulated sugar, salt, orange zest and vanilla, then stir in the fresh orange juice.

Dip the bread slices into the juice mixture, turning them once or twice, until they are thoroughly soaked with the liquid; transfer the slices to a large plate or baking sheet as you work. After all the slices have been soaked, drizzle any remaining liquid over them.

Heat a large griddle or skillet (box, page 55) over medium heat until a few drops of cold water dance when sprinkled on the surface. Cook the slices until the undersides are golden — about three minutes. Turn the slices and cook them until the second sides are lightly browned — two to three minutes more. Transfer the French toast to a clean baking sheet. Brown the remaining slices and transfer them to the baking sheet, too. Bake the French toast until it is cooked through and has puffed up — about 10 minutes.

While the toast is baking, make the orange syrup. Pour 1 cup of water into a small saucepan and stir in the brown sugar; bring the liquid to a boil. Reduce the heat to medium low and simmer the mixture to dissolve the sugar — about one minute. Add the orange-juice concentrate and cook the syrup, stirring, until it is hot — about one minute more. Pour the syrup into a pitcher.

Divide the French toast among eight warmed plates and sprinkle each serving with some of the toasted almonds. Pass the syrup separately.

# Pumpernickel Pancakes

Serves 8
Working (and total) time: about 30 minutes

Calories **157**
Protein **10g.**
Cholesterol **80mg.**
Total fat **3g.**
Saturated fat **1g.**
Sodium **315mg.**

| |
| --- |
| 2 eggs, plus 2 egg whites |
| ⅔ cup low-fat milk |
| 2 large scallions, trimmed and finely chopped |
| ¼ tsp. salt |
| freshly ground black pepper |
| 4 cups fresh pumpernickel bread crumbs (made from about ½ loaf of pumpernickel bread) |
| **Accompaniments** |
| 1 cup yogurt cheese (recipe, page 50) |
| 1 tbsp. red lumpfish caviar |
| 1 scallion, sliced on the diagonal |
| 1 lemon, thinly sliced (optional) |

Whisk together the eggs, egg whites, milk, finely chopped scallions, salt and a generous grinding of pepper in a bowl. Stir in the bread crumbs to make a smooth mixture.

Heat a large griddle or skillet (box, page 55) over medium heat until a few drops of water dance when sprinkled on the surface. Drop the batter 1 generous tablespoon at a time onto the griddle or skillet, and use the back of a spoon to spread the batter into ovals. Cook the pancakes until they are covered with bubbles — one to three minutes. Turn each pancake and cook the second side for one minute more. Transfer the pancakes to a platter and keep them warm while you cook the remaining batter.

Accompany each serving with a dollop of yogurt cheese topped with some caviar and sliced scallions; if you wish, garnish with a slice of lemon.

EDITOR'S NOTE: *Plain low-fat yogurt may be substituted for the yogurt cheese.*

# Griddle Cheesecakes with Cranberry Sauce

Serves 8
Working (and total) time: about 30 minutes

| | |
|---|---|
| Calories **222** | 2 cups low-fat cottage cheese |
| Protein **10g.** | 2 eggs |
| Cholesterol **71mg.** | ¼ cup sugar |
| Total fat **2g.** | 1 cup unbleached all-purpose flour |
| Saturated fat **1g.** | 1 tsp. baking powder |
| Sodium **301mg.** | grated zest of 1 lemon |
| | **Cranberry sauce** |
| | ½ cup sugar |
| | 1 tbsp. cornstarch |
| | 1½ cups fresh orange juice |
| | 2 cups fresh or frozen cranberries, picked over |

To make the cranberry sauce, combine the sugar and cornstarch in a heavy-bottomed saucepan. Gradually pour in the orange juice, stirring continuously. Add the cranberries and bring the mixture to a boil over medium heat, stirring constantly. Reduce the heat and simmer the mixture until all the cranberries have burst — about 15 minutes. Purée the cranberry mixture in a food processor or a blender and then pass it through a sieve into a bowl. Set the sauce aside in a warm place.

Rinse out the food processor or blender and purée the cottage cheese in it. Add the eggs and blend them into the purée. Transfer the mixture to a bowl and stir in the sugar, flour and baking powder, beating just long enough to produce a smooth batter. Stir the lemon zest into the batter.

Heat a large griddle or skillet *(box, page 55)* over medium heat until a few drops of cold water dance when sprinkled on the surface. Drop a generous tablespoon of the batter onto the hot griddle or skillet, and use the back of the spoon to spread the batter to a thickness of ¼ inch. Form several more batter rounds the same way, then cook the griddle cheesecakes until they are covered with bubbles and the undersides are golden — about three minutes. Flip the cheesecakes and cook them until the second sides are lightly browned — about one minute more. Transfer the cheesecakes to a platter and keep them warm while you cook the remaining batter.

Serve the griddle cheesecakes accompanied by the cranberry sauce.

# Paprika Blintzes

Serves 4 as a main dish
Working time: about 50 minutes
Total time: about 1 hour and 30 minutes (includes standing
time for crepe batter)

Calories **223**
Protein **14g.**
Cholesterol **78mg.**
Total fat **10g.**
Saturated fat **3g.**
Sodium **419mg.**

| |
|---|
| ½ cup unbleached all-purpose flour |
| ⅛ tsp. salt |
| 1½ tsp. paprika, preferably Hungarian |
| 1 egg |
| ¾ cup low-fat milk |
| 1 tbsp. olive oil, preferably virgin |
| 1½ tsp. fresh thyme, or ½ tsp. dried thyme leaves |
| ¼ tsp. safflower oil |
| **Cheese-scallion filling** |
| 1½ tsp. olive oil, preferably virgin |
| 1 garlic clove, finely chopped |
| 2 bunches scallions, trimmed and cut into 1-inch pieces |
| 1½ tsp. fresh thyme, or ½ tsp. dried thyme leaves |
| freshly ground black pepper |
| ⅛ tsp. salt |
| ¾ cup low-fat cottage cheese |
| ½ cup plain low-fat yogurt |
| 2 tbsp. freshly grated Parmesan cheese |

To make the crepes for the blintzes, sift the flour, salt and paprika into a bowl. Make a well in the center, then add the egg, milk, olive oil and thyme. Whisk the mixture, gradually incorporating the flour. Cover the bowl and let it stand for one hour, or refrigerate it overnight. If the batter has thickened at the end of the refrigeration period, stir in water, 1 tablespoon at a time, to restore the original consistency.

To make the filling, heat the olive oil in a heavy-bottomed saucepan over medium-high heat. Add the garlic, scallions, thyme, some pepper and the salt. Cook the mixture, stirring frequently, until the scallions are soft — four to five minutes. Transfer the scallion mixture to a bowl.

Put the cottage cheese, the yogurt and the Parmesan cheese into a food processor or a blender and purée them. Add the puréed cheese mixture to the bowl containing the scallions. Stir the cheese-scallion mixture well, then set it aside.

Heat a 6-inch crepe pan or a nonstick skillet over medium-high heat. Add the ¼ teaspoon of safflower oil and spread it over the entire surface with a paper towel. Ladle about 3 tablespoons of the crepe batter into the hot pan and immediately swirl the pan to coat the bottom with a thin, even layer of batter. Pour any excess batter back into the bowl. Cook the crepe until the bottom is browned — about 2 minutes and 30 seconds. Lift the edge with a spatula and turn the crepe over. Cook the crepe on the second side until it, too, is browned — 15 to 30 seconds. Slide the crepe onto a plate. Repeat the process with the remaining batter to form eight crepes in all.

Preheat the oven to 400° F. Spoon about ¼ cup of the cheese-scallion mixture onto a crepe, near its edge. Fold the edge of the crepe over the filling, then fold in the sides of the crepe, forming an envelope around the filling. Roll up the crepe to enclose the filling completely. Repeat the process with the remaining crepes and filling to form eight blintzes. Lightly oil a baking sheet, set the blintzes on it, and bake them until they are crisp and lightly browned around the edges — about eight minutes. Serve the blintzes immediately.

# Buckwheat Crepes with Mushroom-Tomato Filling

Serves 8 as a main dish
Working time: about 1 hour
Total time: about 2 hours
(includes standing time for crepe batter)

Calories **174**
Protein **10g.**
Cholesterol **43mg.**
Total fat **6g.**
Saturated fat **2g.**
Sodium **226mg.**

| |
|---|
| 1 egg |
| 1½ cups low-fat milk |
| ½ tsp. sugar |
| ⅛ tsp. salt |
| 1 tbsp. unsalted butter, melted |
| ½ cup buckwheat flour |
| ½ cup unbleached all-purpose flour |
| ¼ tsp. safflower oil |
| **Mushroom-tomato filling** |
| 1 tbsp. safflower oil |
| 1 lb. mushrooms, wiped clean, trimmed and quartered |
| 2 shallots, thinly sliced |
| 1 tbsp. unbleached all-purpose flour |
| ½ cup unsalted brown stock, or 1 cup unsalted chicken stock reduced by half (recipes, page 138) |
| ¼ cup dry vermouth |
| 4 garlic cloves, finely chopped |
| 2 large tomatoes, peeled, seeded and chopped |
| 1 tbsp. Dijon mustard |
| 2 tbsp. chopped fresh parsley |
| parsley sprigs, for garnish |
| **Creamy cheese topping** |
| 1 cup low-fat cottage cheese |
| 2 tbsp. buttermilk |

Put the egg into a bowl and beat it until it is light and foamy. Whisk in the milk, sugar, salt and butter and then gradually whisk in the two flours. Cover the bowl and let it stand for one hour. (Alternatively, you may refrigerate the batter, covered, overnight.) If the batter has thickened at the end of the refrigeration period, stir in additional milk, 1 tablespoon at a time, until the batter has thinned to its original consistency.

While the batter is resting, make the mushroom-tomato filling. Heat the oil in a heavy-bottomed skillet over medium-high heat. Add the mushrooms and shallots and sauté them until the mushrooms begin to exude their liquid — about five minutes.

Add the flour to the mushrooms and cook the mixture, stirring, for one minute. Add the brown stock or reduced chicken stock, vermouth, garlic and half of the tomatoes; reduce the heat and simmer the mixture for three minutes, stirring frequently. Stir in the mustard and the parsley and remove the pan from the heat.

When the crepe batter is ready, heat a 6-inch crepe

pan or nonstick skillet over medium-high heat. Add the ¼ teaspoon of oil and spread it over the entire surface with a paper towel. Pour about 3 tablespoons of the batter into the hot pan and immediately swirl the pan to coat the bottom with a thin, even layer of batter. Pour any excess batter back into the bowl. Cook the crepe until the bottom is browned — about one minute. Lift the edge with a spatula and turn the crepe over. Cook the crepe on the second side until it, too, is browned — 15 to 30 seconds. Slide the crepe onto a plate. Repeat the process with the remaining batter, brushing the pan lightly with more oil if the crepes begin to stick. Stack the cooked crepes on the plate as you go. Cover the crepes with a towel and set them aside. There should be about 16 crepes.

Preheat the oven to 350° F. Spoon 2 tablespoons of the filling down the center of a crepe. Roll the crepe to enclose the filling, then transfer it to a lightly oiled shallow baking dish. Continue filling and rolling the remaining crepes, transferring them to the baking dish as you work. Bake the filled crepes for 15 minutes.

While the crepes are baking, make the cheese topping. Put the cottage cheese into a food processor or a blender and purée it. Add the buttermilk and process the mixture until it is blended.

Garnish the crepes with the remaining chopped tomato and the parsley sprigs and serve them with the cheese topping.

EDITOR'S NOTE: *Canned beef broth or bouillon may be substituted for the brown stock, but if you do use it, be sure to eliminate the salt from the recipe.*

# Toasted Turkey-and-Provolone Sandwiches with Strawberry-Cranberry Jam

Serves 6 as a main dish
Working (and total) time: about 45 minutes

| | |
|---|---|
| Calories **447** | |
| Protein **31g.** | *12 slices white sandwich bread* |
| Cholesterol **61mg.** | *2 tsp. Dijon mustard* |
| Total fat **12g.** | *¾ lb. sliced roast turkey breast* |
| Saturated fat **6g.** | *6 oz. sliced provolone cheese* |
| Sodium **582mg.** | *1 large red onion, thinly sliced* |
| | *½ cup low-fat milk* |
| | *1 egg white* |
| | *¼ tsp. ground white pepper* |
| | **Strawberry-cranberry jam** |
| | *1 cup fresh or frozen cranberries* |
| | *1 orange, the zest julienned, the juice reserved* |
| | *1 lemon, the zest julienned, the juice reserved* |
| | *½ cup sugar* |
| | *1 cup fresh strawberries, hulled and halved, or frozen whole strawberries, thawed and halved* |

To make the jam, combine the cranberries, orange zest and juice, lemon zest and juice, and sugar in a nonreactive saucepan. Bring the mixture to a boil, reduce the heat, and simmer the fruit for five minutes. Add the strawberries to the saucepan, stir well, and cook the jam for an additional five minutes. Transfer the jam to a bowl and chill it.

Preheat the oven to 350° F.

Lay 6 of the bread slices out on a work surface and brush them with the mustard. Divide the turkey, provolone cheese and onion among these 6 slices. Set the remaining slices of bread on top.

In a small bowl, whisk together the milk, egg white and pepper. Brush both sides of the sandwiches with this mixture. Heat a large griddle or skillet *(box, page 55)* over medium heat until a few drops of cold water dance when sprinkled on the surface. Put the sandwiches on the griddle or in the skillet and cook them until the undersides are well browned — about five minutes. Turn the sandwiches and cook them until the second sides are browned — two to three minutes more. Serve the sandwiches immediately, accompanied by the jam.

# Puffy Fruit Omelet

Serves 4 as a main dish
Working ( and total) time: about 40 minutes

Calories **200**
Protein **10g.**
Cholesterol **139mg.**
Total fat **5g.**
Saturated fat **1g.**
Sodium **250mg.**

| |
|---|
| 2 eggs, separated, plus 2 egg whites |
| 2 tbsp. unbleached all-purpose flour |
| ½ tsp. baking powder |
| ⅛ tsp. salt |
| ½ cup low-fat milk |
| 5 tsp. sugar |
| 1 tsp. safflower oil |
| 1 sweet red apple, preferably Stayman or Winesap, quartered, cored and cut into ½-inch pieces |
| 1 pear, preferably Bosc, quartered, cored and cut into ½-inch pieces |
| 1 tsp. fresh lemon juice |
| ¼ tsp. ground cinnamon |
| 2 tbsp. raspberry preserves |
| 2 tbsp. apple cider or unsweetened apple juice |

Preheat the oven to 450° F. In a bowl, whisk together the egg yolks, flour, baking powder, salt and 3 tablespoons of the milk until the mixture is well blended — five to seven minutes. Whisk in the remaining milk.

In another bowl, beat the egg whites with 3 teaspoons of the sugar until they form soft peaks. Stir half of the whites into the yolk mixture and then gently fold in the remaining whites just until the mixture is blended; do not overmix. Set the egg mixture aside.

Heat the oil in a large, ovenproof skillet over medium-high heat. Add the apple and the pear, the remaining 2 teaspoons of sugar, the lemon juice and the cinnamon and cook the fruit, stirring frequently, until it is tender — about five minutes. Remove the skillet from the heat and pour the egg mixture over the fruit; smooth the top of the mixture with a spatula. Place the skillet in the oven and bake the omelet until the top is golden brown — 10 to 15 minutes.

While the omelet is baking, mix together the raspberry preserves and the cider or unsweetened apple juice in a small dish. When the omelet is ready, drizzle this syrup over it, slice it into quarters and serve the omelet immediately.

## Frittata with Mozzarella Cheese

Serves 4 as a main dish
Working (and total) time: about 35 minutes

Calories **170**
Protein **11g.**
Cholesterol **83mg.**
Total fat **11g.**
Saturated fat **4g.**
Sodium **320mg.**

| |
|---|
| 1 egg, plus 2 egg whites |
| ¼ tsp. salt |
| freshly ground black pepper |
| ¼ cup part-skim ricotta cheese |
| 1½ tbsp. olive oil, preferably virgin |
| 3 oz. mushrooms (about 1 cup), wiped clean and sliced |
| 2 garlic cloves, finely chopped |
| 1½ tsp. fresh thyme, or ½ tsp. dried thyme leaves |
| 3 scallions, trimmed and cut into ½-inch pieces, the white and green parts separated |
| 2 small zucchini (about ½ lb.), cut into bâtons |
| 1 sweet red pepper, seeded, deribbed and sliced into thin strips |
| 1½ tsp. fresh lemon juice |
| 2 tbsp. freshly grated Parmesan cheese |
| 2 oz. part-skim mozzarella, cut into thin strips (about ¼ cup) |

In a bowl, whisk together the egg, egg whites, ⅛ teaspoon of the salt, some pepper, the ricotta and ½ tablespoon of the oil and set the mixture aside.

Preheat the broiler. Heat the remaining tablespoon of oil in a large, ovenproof, nonstick skillet over high heat. Add the mushrooms, garlic, thyme, the white parts of the scallion and some pepper. Cook the vegetable mixture until the mushrooms are lightly browned — two to three minutes. Add the zucchini, red pepper, the remaining ⅛ teaspoon of salt and the lemon juice, and cook the mixture, stirring frequently, until the vegetables are tender and all of the liquid has evaporated — about five minutes.

Remove the skillet from the heat and stir the scallion greens and the Parmesan cheese into the vegetable mixture. Press the vegetables into an even layer and pour in the egg mixture. Cook the frittata over medium heat for one minute. Sprinkle the mozzarella evenly over the frittata and place the skillet under the preheated broiler. Broil the frittata until the cheese begins to brown — two to three minutes. Slide the frittata onto a warm serving plate and cut it into quarters. Serve the frittata immediately.

## Omelets Stuffed with Seafood and Sprouts

Serves 4
Working (and total) time: about 35 minutes

Calories **158**
Protein **13g.**
Cholesterol **106mg.**
Total fat **8g.**
Saturated fat **1g.**
Sodium **86mg.**

| |
|---|
| 3 tbsp. rice vinegar |
| 3 tsp. sugar |
| 1 tbsp. fresh lemon juice |
| ½ lb. bean sprouts |
| ¼ lb. green beans, trimmed and thinly sliced on the diagonal |
| 1 tbsp. plus 2 tsp. safflower oil |
| 1 tsp. curry powder |
| freshly ground black pepper |
| 2 oz. cooked baby shrimp (about ⅓ cup), chopped |
| ¼ lb. sole or flounder fillets, cut into strips |
| 2 scallions, thinly sliced |
| 1 egg, plus 3 egg whites |

Mix the vinegar, 2 teaspoons of the sugar and the lemon juice in a small bowl and set it aside.

Blanch the bean sprouts and the beans in 1 quart of boiling water for 30 seconds. Drain the vegetables and refresh them under cold running water. Squeeze the vegetables in your hands to extract as much liquid as possible. Set the vegetables aside.

Heat 1 teaspoon of the oil in a large, nonstick skillet over medium-high heat. Add the bean sprouts and beans and cook them, stirring frequently, for two minutes. Add ½ teaspoon of the curry, half of the vinegar mixture and a generous grinding of black pepper. Stir the mixture well and continue cooking it until all of the liquid has evaporated — about two minutes. Transfer the vegetable mixture to a bowl and set it aside.

Return the skillet to the heat and pour in 1 tablespoon of the oil. Add the shrimp, sole or flounder, and scallions and cook the mixture, stirring frequently, for one minute. Add the remaining vinegar mixture, then ▶

stir in the vegetable mixture, and cook them, stirring frequently, until all of the liquid has evaporated — two to four minutes. Set the seafood and vegetables aside.

In a bowl, whisk together the egg, egg whites, the remaining ½ teaspoon of curry, the remaining teaspoon of sugar, the remaining teaspoon of oil and some pepper. With a paper towel, wipe out the nonstick skillet that the seafood and vegetables were cooked in and heat the skillet over medium heat. Pour a scant ¼ cup of the egg mixture into the hot skillet and swirl it around. Cook the omelet for 30 seconds, turn it over, and cook it for 10 seconds more. Transfer the omelet to a warm plate. Repeat the process with the remaining egg mixture to make four thin omelets.

Take one fourth of the filling and spread it over one half of one omelet. Fold the omelet over and repeat the process with the remaining omelets and filling. Serve the filled omelets immediately.

# Turkey, Apple and Champagne Sausages

Serves 10 as a main dish
Working (and total) time: about 45 minutes

Calories **109**
Protein **14g.**
Cholesterol **32mg.**
Total fat **2g.**
Saturated fat **1g.**
Sodium **162mg.**

| |
|---|
| 1 red apple, cored and finely chopped |
| 1 onion, finely chopped |
| 1 cup fine dry bread crumbs |
| ½ cup dry Champagne or other sparkling dry white wine |
| 1 lb. turkey breast meat, ground |
| ¼ lb. pork loin, trimmed of fat and ground |
| ½ tsp. salt |
| freshly ground black pepper |

Put the apple and onion into a nonstick skillet over low heat and cook them, covered, until they are soft — about four minutes.

Combine the bread crumbs and the wine in a bowl. Add the turkey, pork, salt, some pepper and the apple-onion mixture, kneading the ingredients with your hands to mix them well. Shape the sausage meat into 20 patties about ½ inch thick.

Heat a large, nonstick skillet over medium heat and put half the patties into it. Cook them until the undersides are brown, then turn the patties over, and brown the other sides — about four minutes in all. Remove the browned patties to a platter and keep them warm while you cook the others. Serve the sausages at once.

# Spaghetti Omelet

Serves 8 as a side dish
Working (and total) time: about 1 hour

Calories **121**
Protein **7g.**
Cholesterol **6mg.**
Total fat **3g.**
Saturated fat **1g.**
Sodium **262mg.**

| |
|---|
| 28 oz. canned unsalted whole tomatoes, with their juice |
| 4 oz. spaghetti, spaghettini or linguine |
| 1½ tsp. salt |
| 2 egg whites |
| ½ cup low-fat milk |
| 1 tbsp. chopped fresh parsley |
| 3 tbsp. freshly grated Parmesan cheese |
| freshly ground black pepper |
| 1 tsp. grated lemon zest |
| 2 tsp. olive oil |
| ½ cup grated part-skim mozzarella cheese |

Put the tomatoes and their juice into a heavy-bottomed, nonreactive saucepan. Simmer the mixture, stirring it occasionally to prevent it from sticking, until it thickens — 20 to 30 minutes.

While the tomatoes are cooking, prepare the pasta. Add the pasta to 2 quarts of boiling water with 1 teaspoon of the salt. Start testing the pasta after eight minutes and cook it until it is *al dente*. Drain the cooked pasta, rinse it under cold running water and drain it again, thoroughly.

In a large bowl, beat together the egg whites, milk, parsley, Parmesan, a generous grinding of pepper, the remaining ½ teaspoon of salt and the lemon zest. Toss the pasta with the egg-white mixture.

Heat a 9-inch nonstick skillet over medium-high heat. Add the oil, let it heat for 10 seconds and then swirl the pan to evenly coat the bottom with the oil. Put half of the pasta mixture into the skillet; use a rubber spatula to smooth the mixture into an even layer. Reduce the heat to medium. Sprinkle the mozzarella over the pasta mixture and cover it with the remaining mixture. Let the omelet cook slowly until it is firm and the bottom and sides are browned — about eight minutes.

Slide the omelet onto a plate. Invert the skillet over the plate and turn both over together. Cook the second side until it, too, is browned — approximately eight minutes longer.

While the omelet is cooking, make the tomato sauce: Work the cooked tomatoes through a food mill or a sieve and discard the seeds. Keep the tomato sauce warm.

To serve the omelet, slide it onto a warmed serving platter. Cut the omelet into eight wedges and serve it immediately, passing the tomato sauce separately.

# Greek-Style Chicken and Rice Casserole

Serves 8 as a main dish
Working time: about 30 minutes
Total time: about 1 hour

Calories **276**
Protein **17g.**
Cholesterol **52mg.**
Total fat **11g.**
Saturated fat **3g.**
Sodium **244mg.**

| |
| --- |
| 2 tbsp. safflower oil |
| 8 chicken thighs, skinned |
| 1 cup rice |
| 1 onion, chopped |
| 4 garlic cloves, finely chopped |
| 1 cup unsalted chicken stock (recipe, page 138) |
| 28 oz. canned unsalted whole tomatoes |
| 3 tbsp. chopped fresh oregano, or 2 tsp. dried oregano |
| 1 tbsp. fresh thyme, or 1 tsp. dried thyme leaves |
| 12 oil-cured olives, pitted and quartered, or 12 pitted black olives, coarsely chopped |
| 1 oz. feta cheese, rinsed and crumbled (about ¼ cup) |

Heat the oil in a large, heavy-bottomed casserole over medium-high heat. Add four of the thighs and cook them until they are lightly browned — about four minutes on each side. Remove the first four thighs and brown the other four. Set all the thighs aside.

Reduce the heat to medium and add the rice, onion, garlic and ¼ cup of the stock. Cook the mixture, stirring constantly, until the onion is translucent — about four minutes. Add the remaining ¾ cup of stock, the tomatoes, the oregano and the thyme. Push the thighs down into the rice mixture. Bring the liquid to a boil, reduce the heat, and simmer the chicken, tightly covered, until the rice is tender — 20 to 30 minutes.

Stir the olives into the chicken and rice, and serve the casserole with the feta cheese on top.

# Lean Beef Sausages

Serves 4 as a main dish
Working time: about 20 minutes
Total time: about 40 minutes

Calories **99**
Protein **14g.**
Cholesterol **36mg.**
Total fat **4g.**
Saturated fat **1g.**
Sodium **124mg.**

| |
|---|
| ½ lb. beef round, trimmed of fat and ground |
| ½ cup unsalted brown stock (recipe, page 138) |
| 2 tbsp. fresh bread crumbs |
| ½ tsp. grated lemon zest |
| ½ tsp. finely chopped garlic |
| 1 tsp. chopped fresh sage, or ¼ tsp. crumbled dried sage |
| ½ tsp. paprika |
| 1 egg white |
| ⅛ tsp. salt |
| freshly ground black pepper |

In a large bowl, mix together the beef, brown stock, bread crumbs, lemon zest, garlic, sage, paprika, egg white, salt and some pepper.

Arrange half of the beef mixture in a line on a piece of heavy-duty plastic wrap about 12 inches long. Form one sausage following the technique shown on page 77. Using the remaining meat mixture, shape a second sausage.

Pour enough water into a large pot to fill it about 1 inch deep. Set a vegetable steamer in the pot and put the sausages into it. Cover the pot and bring the water to a boil. Steam the sausages until they are firm — seven to 10 minutes. Remove the steamer from the pot and let the sausages cool in the plastic wrap. Remove the wrap from the sausages and cut them in half crosswise.

Heat a nonstick skillet over medium-high heat, put the sausages into the skillet and cook them until they are well browned on all sides — four to five minutes in all. Serve the sausages at once.

EDITOR'S NOTE: *Canned beef broth or bouillon may be substituted for the brown stock, but if you do use it, be sure to omit the salt from the recipe.*

## Making Sausage

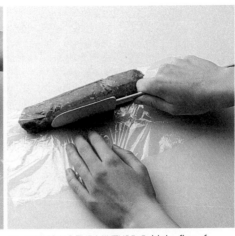

1 *SHAPING THE MEAT. Lay a piece of heavy-duty plastic wrap on the work surface. Place the prepared meat mixture in the amount specified in the recipe near the edge of the wrap. Pat the meat into a cylindrical shape with a spatula.*

2 *WRAPPING THE MIXTURE. Fold the flap of plastic over the sausage. Holding the spatula against the edge of the meat, exert pressure to force out extra air and to compact the sausage. Roll the bundle forward, wrapping up the sausage as you go.*

3 *TYING THE ENDS. To help the sausage hold its shape and to prevent water from seeping into it during the cooking, twist and tie the two ends of the plastic wrap with butcher's twine.*

# Lentil and Curly Endive Salad

Serves 8 as a side dish
Working time: about 20 minutes
Total time: about 1 hour

Calories **117**
Protein **6g.**
Cholesterol **0mg.**
Total fat **3g.**
Saturated fat **0g.**
Sodium **76mg.**

| |
|---|
| *2 ripe tomatoes, halved, seeded and cut into ½-inch pieces* |
| *½ lb. lentils, picked over (about 1 cup)* |
| *¼ tsp. salt* |
| *freshly ground black pepper* |
| *1 ½ tbsp. olive oil, preferably virgin* |
| *½ head of curly endive (chicory), washed, dried and sliced into 1-inch pieces (about 4 cups)* |
| *1 tsp. honey* |
| *¼ cup red wine vinegar* |

Put the tomatoes into a strainer and let them drain; set the strainer aside.

Rinse the lentils and put them into a saucepan with 4 cups of water. Bring the water to a boil, then reduce the heat, and simmer the lentils until they are tender — 25 to 40 minutes. Drain the lentils and then transfer them to a bowl. Toss them with the salt and some pepper and set the bowl aside.

Heat ½ tablespoon of the oil in a large, heavy-bottomed skillet over high heat. Add the endive and some pepper and cook the mixture, stirring constantly, just until the endive has wilted — about one minute. Put the endive into the strainer with the tomatoes.

Whisk the remaining tablespoon of oil, the honey, vinegar and some pepper in a large bowl. Add the tomatoes, endive and lentils and toss the salad well. You may serve the salad immediately or let it cool to room temperature.

# Four-Vegetable Kasha Salad

Serves 8 as a side dish
Working time: about 30 minutes
Total time: about 45 minutes

Calories **99**
Protein **4g.**
Cholesterol **0mg.**
Total fat **4g.**
Saturated fat **1g.**
Sodium **67mg.**

| |
| --- |
| 1 cup whole kasha (toasted buckwheat groats) |
| 1 egg white |
| 2 tbsp. olive oil |
| ⅛ tsp. salt |
| 2 cups unsalted chicken stock (recipe, page 138) or water |
| 1½ lb. fresh green peas, shelled, or 1½ cups frozen baby peas, thawed |
| 1 sweet red pepper, seeded, deribbed and cut into ½-inch pieces |
| 3 scallions, trimmed and cut on the diagonal into ½-inch pieces |
| ½ cup diced celery |
| ¼ tsp. cayenne pepper |
| 3 tbsp. sherry vinegar or red wine vinegar |

Mix the kasha with the egg white in a small bowl. Heat ½ tablespoon of the oil in a large, heavy-bottomed saucepan over medium heat. Add the moistened kasha to the saucepan, and cook it, stirring constantly, until the kasha grains have separated and the mixture is dry — about three minutes. Add the salt and the stock or water. Bring the mixture to a boil, reduce the heat, and simmer the kasha, covered, until all of the liquid is absorbed and the kasha is tender — approximately 20 minutes.

While the kasha is cooking, prepare the vegetables. If you are using fresh peas, boil them until they are tender — five to seven minutes. (Frozen peas do not require cooking for this recipe.) Drain the peas and put them, along with the red pepper, scallions, celery and cayenne pepper, into a large serving bowl. Stir in the vinegar and the remaining 1½ tablespoons of oil. When the kasha is ready, add it to the vegetables and toss the salad well. The salad may be served at room temperature or chilled.

## Broccoli and Ricotta Pie

Serves 6 as a main dish
Working time: about 1 hour
Total time: about 2 hours

Calories **325**
Protein **17g.**
Cholesterol **63mg.**
Total fat **8g.**
Saturated fat **3g.**
Sodium **284mg.**

| |
|---|
| 1 envelope fast-rising dry yeast (about 1 tbsp.) |
| 2½ cups bread flour |
| ¼ tsp. salt |
| 1 tbsp. olive oil, preferably virgin |
| 1½ cups chopped onion |
| ½ tsp. caraway seeds, or 2 tsp. dried dill |
| 1 egg, plus 2 egg whites |
| ¾ cup part-skim ricotta cheese |
| ¾ cup low-fat milk |
| freshly ground black pepper |
| ⅛ tsp. grated nutmeg |
| 1 oz. Canadian bacon, finely chopped |
| 1 tbsp. cornmeal |
| 1½ cups broccoli florets, blanched in boiling water for one minute, drained |
| 2 tbsp. freshly grated Parmesan cheese |

In a large bowl, mix the yeast with 1 cup of the flour and ⅛ teaspoon of the salt. Heat ¾ cup of water in a saucepan just until it is hot to the touch (130° F.). Pour the hot water into the flour mixture and stir the dough vigorously with a wooden spoon. Stir in 1 teaspoon of the oil and 1 more cup of the flour. Transfer the dough to a floured surface and begin to knead it. If the dough seems too sticky, gradually add up to ½ cup of flour; if it seems too dry, add water, 1 teaspoon at a time, as required. Knead the dough until it is smooth and elastic — about 10 minutes. Transfer the dough to an oiled bowl, turn the dough once to coat it with the oil, and cover the bowl with a damp towel or plastic wrap. Set the bowl in a warm, draft-free place and let the dough rise until it has doubled in volume — about 30 minutes.

While the dough is rising, heat the remaining 2 teaspoons of oil in a heavy-bottomed skillet over medium-high heat. Add the onion and the caraway seeds or dill and cook the mixture, stirring frequently, until the onion is lightly browned — about 10 minutes. Remove the skillet from the heat and set it aside.

Whisk the egg and the egg whites in a large bowl. Whisk in the ricotta, the milk, the remaining ⅛ teaspoon of salt, some pepper, the nutmeg and the Canadian bacon. Stir in half of the onion mixture and set the bowl aside.

Preheat the oven to 400° F. After the dough has finished rising, punch it down. Knead the remaining onion mixture into the dough.

Sprinkle an 8-inch-wide cast-iron skillet or an 11-inch glass pie plate with the cornmeal. Put the dough in the skillet or pie plate and, with your fingertips, gently work some of the dough toward the edge to form a 2-inch-high rim. Allow the dough to stand for 10 minutes.

Place the skillet or pie plate in the oven for 10 minutes to partially bake the dough. Remove the crust from the oven; if the edge is not ¾ of an inch higher than the flat surface of the crust, gently push the dough down to form a depression. Pour in the ricotta-egg mixture. Place the broccoli florets one at a time, bud sides up, in the filling, then sprinkle the Parmesan cheese over the surface of the pie. Return the skillet to the oven and bake the pie until the filling is set and the top is lightly browned — 35 to 40 minutes. Let the pie stand for 10 minutes before cutting it into wedges.

## Braised Endive and Red Pepper Salad

Serves 6 as a side dish
Working time: about 30 minutes
Total time: about 2 hours (includes chilling)

Calories **38**
Protein **1g.**
Cholesterol **0mg.**
Total fat **2g.**
Saturated fat **0g.**
Sodium **108mg.**

| |
| --- |
| *2 sweet red peppers* |
| *1 tbsp. olive oil, preferably virgin* |
| *4 heads of Belgian endive (about 1 lb.), trimmed and cut into 1-inch pieces* |
| *1 tbsp. fresh thyme, or 1 tsp. dried thyme leaves* |
| *1 tbsp. fresh lemon juice* |
| *¼ tsp. salt* |
| *3 scallions, trimmed and cut into 1-inch pieces* |
| *freshly ground black pepper* |
| *2 tbsp. sherry vinegar, or 1 ½ tbsp. red wine vinegar* |

To prepare the peppers, place them about 2 inches below a preheated broiler. Broil the peppers, turning them as their sides become scorched, until their skin has blistered all over. Transfer the peppers to a bowl and cover it with plastic wrap, or put them in a paper bag and fold it shut; the trapped steam will make the peppers limp and loosen their skins — about 15 minutes. With a paring knife, peel off the peppers' skins in sections, peeling from top to bottom. Remove the stems, ribs and seeds from the peppers, working over a bowl to catch the juices. Strain the pepper juices into another bowl and set it aside. Slice the peppers lengthwise into ½-inch-wide, 2-inch-long strips and add them to the juices.

Heat the oil in a large, heavy-bottomed skillet over medium heat. Add the endive and the thyme and cook the mixture, stirring constantly, until the endive begins to wilt — about five minutes. Stir in the lemon juice, salt, scallions and some pepper, then cook the mixture for three minutes more, stirring frequently. Add the peppers with their juices and the vinegar; continue cooking for two minutes. Scrape the contents of the skillet into a bowl, then refrigerate the salad until it is cool — about one hour and 30 minutes. The salad may be served chilled or at room temperature.

EDITOR'S NOTE: *This dish can be made a day in advance and refrigerated until serving time.*

# Layered Bread, Tomato and Zucchini Casserole

Serves 8 as a main dish
Working time: about 1 hour
Total time: about 1½ hours

Calories **200**
Protein **12g.**
Cholesterol **78mg.**
Total fat **5g.**
Saturated fat **2g.**
Sodium **376mg.**

| |
|---|
| 2 eggs, plus 2 egg whites |
| 1 cup low-fat milk |
| ¼ tsp. salt |
| freshly ground black pepper |
| 2 small zucchini, or 1 large zucchini, cut into ¼-inch-thick rounds (about ½ lb.) |
| 1 onion, chopped |
| 4 ripe tomatoes, peeled, seeded and chopped, or 14 oz. canned unsalted whole tomatoes, drained and chopped |
| ¼ cup chopped fresh parsley |
| 2 tbsp. chopped fresh basil, or 2 tsp. dried basil |
| 8 slices Italian or French bread, cut into ½-inch cubes (about 8 cups) |
| ¼ lb. part-skim mozzarella cheese, grated (about 1 cup) |

Whisk the eggs, egg whites, milk, salt and some pepper together in a bowl and set it aside. Preheat the oven to 350° F.

Put the zucchini and onion into a nonstick skillet over low heat and cook them, covered, until they are soft — about four minutes. Add the tomatoes and increase the heat to high. Cook the vegetables, stirring continuously, until most of the liquid has evaporated — about five minutes. Remove the skillet from the heat and stir in the parsley and basil.

Spoon half of the vegetable mixture into an 8-by-12-inch baking dish; add half of the bread cubes and sprinkle half of the cheese over the bread. Repeat the process with the remaining vegetable mixture, bread and cheese, then pour the egg mixture over all.

Bake the casserole until the egg mixture has set — about 20 minutes. Increase the oven temperature to 450° F. and continue baking the casserole until it is lightly browned — about five minutes more. Cut the casserole into eight squares and serve it hot.

# Tomato Soufflé

Serves 4 as a main dish or 8 as a side dish
Working time: about 40 minutes
Total time: about 1 hour and 40 minutes

| | |
|---|---|
| Calories **189** | 2 large new potatoes (about ¾ lb.), peeled and quartered |
| Protein **9g.** | 14 oz. canned unsalted whole tomatoes, seeded, the juice reserved |
| Cholesterol **69mg.** | |
| Total fat **5g.** | 1 tsp. sugar |
| Saturated fat **1g.** | 1 onion, chopped |
| Sodium **220mg.** | 1½ tbsp. chopped fresh ginger |
| | 2 garlic cloves, finely chopped |
| | 1 ripe tomato |
| | 2 tbsp. unbleached all-purpose flour |
| | 1 egg, separated, plus 4 egg whites |
| | ¼ tsp. salt |
| | freshly ground black pepper |
| | 1 tbsp. olive oil |

Put the potatoes into a saucepan, cover them with water, and bring it to a boil. Cook the potatoes until they are tender — 15 to 20 minutes. Drain the potatoes and return them to the saucepan.

Preheat the oven to 450° F.

Add the canned tomatoes and their juice, the sugar, onion, ginger and garlic to the potatoes and bring the mixture to a boil. Reduce the heat and simmer the mixture, stirring frequently, until it has thickened and most of the liquid has evaporated — 15 to 20 minutes.

While the tomato mixture is simmering, prepare the fresh tomato. With a small sharp knife, cut the flesh of the tomato away from the seeds and core. Discard the seeds and core. Then cut the flesh into ¼-inch dice and put it into a large bowl. Lightly oil a 1½-quart soufflé dish and add the flour. Invert the dish and shake out the excess flour.

Transfer the cooked tomato mixture to a food processor or a blender and purée it. Pour the purée into the bowl with the diced tomato and stir in the egg yolk, salt, some pepper and the olive oil. Set the bowl aside.

Beat the egg whites in a bowl until they form soft peaks. Stir about one fourth of the beaten whites into the tomato mixture to lighten it. Gently fold in the remaining whites just until they are blended in.

Pour the soufflé mixture into the prepared dish and bake it until the soufflé has risen and the top is dark brown — 30 to 40 minutes. Serve the soufflé immediately.

# Cheddar and Vegetable Phyllo Roll

Serves 6 as a side dish
Working time: about 40 minutes
Total time: about 1 hour and 15 minutes

Calories **143**
Protein **6g.**
Cholesterol **7mg.**
Total fat **6g.**
Saturated fat **2g.**
Sodium **162mg.**

| |
|---|
| 2 cups broccoli florets |
| 4 tsp. safflower oil |
| 1 shallot, finely chopped (about 2 tbsp.) |
| 1 yellow squash, halved, seeded, the flesh grated |
| ⅓ cup dry vermouth |
| 2 tbsp. flour |
| ½ cup low-fat milk |
| 1 oz. Cheddar cheese, grated (about ¼ cup) |
| ⅛ tsp. salt |
| 4 sheets phyllo dough (about 1 ½ oz.) |

Pour enough water into a saucepan to fill it 1 inch deep. Set a vegetable steamer in the pan and bring the water to a boil. Put the broccoli into the steamer, cover the pan tightly, and steam the broccoli until it is tender — about seven minutes. When the broccoli has cooled, chop it coarsely and set it aside.

Preheat the oven to 425° F. Heat 2 teaspoons of the oil in a large, nonstick skillet over medium-high heat. Add the shallot and sauté it until it is translucent — about two minutes. Add the yellow squash and cook it, stirring continuously, until it is tender — about two minutes more. Reduce the heat to medium, add the broccoli and vermouth to the vegetables, and cook them until the vermouth has evaporated — approximately five minutes.

Stir the flour into the vegetables. Add the milk and continue cooking the mixture, stirring continuously, until the liquid comes to a boil. Add the cheese and salt and set the skillet aside to cool.

Place the phyllo sheets, stacked on top of each other, on a work surface. Spoon the cooled vegetable mixture lengthwise down the center of the top sheet. Fold a long side of the stack of sheets over the filling

and brush the edge lightly with some of the oil. Fold the other long side over to cover the filling.

Brush both ends with about 1 teaspoon of the remaining oil. Fold up the ends to enclose the filling. Turn the phyllo roll seam side down and set it onto a baking sheet. Brush the top surface with the remaining oil. Bake the roll until the phyllo is crisp — approximately 20 minutes.

2

# Brunches for All Occasions

Like a good piece of music, a successful meal is a harmonious composition: Tastes, textures, colors and shapes combine to heighten the pleasure inherent in each individual dish. A brunch demands something more — delicious lightness. And so the 10 menus presented in this chapter are designed to satisfy your guests or family without overwhelming them with rich foods or too large a number of dishes that demand sampling and encourage indulgence. The menus all are low enough in calories to allow you to supplement the dishes, if you like, with bread, rice or potatoes.

A central idea helps give each of these menus coherence. Four are based on culinary traditions — Chinese, British, Scandinavian and American Southwest. Four others are inspired by the seasons and the special foods then at their prime. The spring brunch, for instance, features asparagus, which is at its fleeting, succulent best from March to May. The sturdier fall menu reflects the return of cool weather and a bountiful harvest of apples, sweet potatoes, cabbage, chestnuts and pears. The style of entertaining determines the choice of dishes for the remaining two menus, a picnic brunch and a buffet for a large group. In fact, almost all of the menus are well suited to the casual service that a buffet offers. But they could also do double duty as a sit-down meal.

Since brunches take place relatively early in the day, the menus that follow consist of dishes that for the most part can be prepared partially or completely a day or even more in advance. But make sure your refrigerator or freezer has room to accommodate the dishes, as well as any ingredients you will have to prepare the day of the brunch.

These menus may be freely varied, according to your needs or your imagination. The Scandinavian menu, for example, provides a trio of salads, but if you are serving six people instead of the eight for which the brunch is designed, you may simply omit one of the salads. To eliminate the last-minute flurry of cooking that a stovetop bread requires, you could replace the corn griddlecakes of the Southwestern menu with the spicy corn-bread sticks included in the first section *(page 31)*. You may also have favorite recipes from other sources that would marry well with the ones that appear here. And, if you like, you can always lift a recipe or two from any of these menus to include in a brunch of your own devising.

---

*Unpacked on a grassy spot, an unhurried brunch awaits picnickers. A spinach roulade is served with eggplant relish and green beans, and peach compote with orange-walnut cake and raspberry iced tea complete the meal.*

### PICNIC BRUNCH

*Apple-Mushroom Spinach Roulade*
*Eggplant-and-Pepper Relish*
*Green Beans with Garlic and Canadian Bacon*
*Fresh Peach Compote*
*Orange-Walnut Coffeecake*
*Raspberry Iced Tea*

The day before this picnic brunch, bake the orange-walnut coffeecake and the spinach spongecake for the roulade. Prepare the filling, and fill, roll and wrap the roulade. Make the eggplant relish and the peach dessert. Prepare the bean salad to the point of adding the tomatoes. Wrap or tightly cover all the dishes. Make the raspberry tea, and refrigerate everything.

On the next day, slice the roulade, the coffeecake and the tomato garnish for the green-bean salad. Pack the spinach garnish for the roulade, and put the salad, the compote and the relish into pretty containers with lids. Pack a platter for the roulade and a napkin-lined container for the cake. Pour the chilled tea into a thermos and, if you like, take along some ice cubes.

# Apple-Mushroom Spinach Roulade

Serves 8
Working time: about 1 hour and 15 minutes
Total time: about 1 hour and 45 minutes

Calories **124**
Protein **7g.**
Cholesterol **73mg.**
Total fat **5g.**
Saturated fat **1g.**
Sodium **269mg.**

| |
|---|
| ¾ lb. spinach, washed and stemmed, or 5 oz. frozen spinach |
| ½ cup cake flour |
| ¼ cup whole-wheat flour |
| 1 tsp. baking powder |
| ½ tsp. ground mace |
| ¼ tsp. salt |
| freshly ground black pepper |
| 2 egg yolks |
| 4 egg whites |
| **Apple-mushroom filling** |
| 1 large onion, finely chopped |
| 2 apples, peeled, cored and chopped |
| ½ lb. mushrooms, wiped clean and thinly sliced |
| ¼ tsp. salt |
| freshly ground black pepper |
| ½ cup part-skim ricotta cheese |

Line a 12-by-16-inch jelly-roll pan with parchment or wax paper. Lightly butter the paper, then dust it with flour; shake off the excess flour. Set the pan aside.

If you are using fresh spinach, reserve 10 of the leaves for garnish; put the remaining leaves into a large, heavy-bottomed skillet and cook them over medium heat, stirring occasionally, just until they wilt —

about three minutes. (The water clinging to the leaves provides enough moisture.) Transfer the spinach to a colander and let it cool. If you are using frozen spinach, thaw it but do not cook it.

Squeeze the spinach into a ball to extract as much liquid as possible. Purée the spinach in a food processor or chop it very finely by hand. Set the spinach aside.

Sift together the cake flour, whole-wheat flour, baking powder, mace, salt and pepper into a small bowl. In another bowl, beat the egg yolks with an electric mixer on high until they are thick — about four minutes. Bring ¼ cup of water to a boil in a small saucepan; gradually pour the water into the egg yolks, beating continuously. Beat the yolks on high speed until they are pale and very fluffy; gently stir in the spinach.

Preheat the oven to 350° F. In another bowl, beat the egg whites until they form soft peaks. Fold the flour mixture into the spinach-egg-yolk mixture, and then fold in the egg whites.

Spread the batter out evenly on the prepared pan. Bake the spinach spongecake until it is set but still tender and moist — eight to 10 minutes. Remove the spongecake from the oven and loosen the edges with the tip of a knife. Cover the cake with a damp towel.

While the spongecake is cooling, make the apple-mushroom filling. Cook the onion and the apples, covered, in a large, nonstick skillet over low heat until the apples are very soft — about 20 minutes. Add the mushrooms and continue to cook the mixture, still covered, until the mushrooms have released their juice — about five minutes more. Remove the cover, increase the heat to medium high, and stir in the salt and some pepper. Simmer the mixture until almost all of the liquid has evaporated — about three minutes. The filling should be moist but not wet. Remove the skillet from the heat. With a wooden spoon, push the ricotta through a sieve held over the skillet; stir the mixture thoroughly.

To assemble the roulade, invert the jelly-roll pan so that the towel is on the bottom. Lift away the pan and peel off the paper. Spread the apple-mushroom filling onto the cake, leaving a ½-inch border all around. Starting at a long side, roll the spongecake into a tight cylinder, using the towel to help guide the rolling process. Trim the ends, wrap the roulade tightly in aluminum foil, and refrigerate it. When you are ready to serve the roulade, slice it and arrange it on a platter garnished with the reserved spinach leaves.

# Eggplant-and-Pepper Relish

Serves 8
Working (and total) time: about 45 minutes

Calories **17**
Protein **0g.**
Cholesterol **0mg.**
Total fat **1g.**
Saturated fat **0g.**
Sodium **14mg.**

| |
|---|
| 2 sweet red peppers |
| 1 tsp. safflower oil |
| ½ lb. eggplant, cut into 2-inch julienne |
| 1 cup finely chopped celery |
| ¼ tsp. celery seeds |
| ¼ tsp. ground coriander |
| ⅛ tsp. cayenne pepper |
| 2 tbsp. cider vinegar |

Roast the peppers under a preheated broiler, turning them with tongs as they blister, until their skins are blackened all over — about 15 minutes. Transfer the peppers to a bowl and cover it with plastic wrap; the trapped steam will loosen the peppers' skins. When the peppers are cool enough to handle, peel, seed and derib them. Cut the peppers into julienne strips and set them aside.

Heat the oil in a large, nonstick skillet over medium-high heat. Add the eggplant and celery, cooking them until they are soft and lightly browned — about five minutes. Take the skillet off the heat and stir in the red pepper julienne, celery seeds, coriander, cayenne pepper and vinegar. Let the relish cool completely and spoon it into a serving dish. Serve the relish at room temperature.

# Green Beans with Garlic and Canadian Bacon

Serves 8
Working time: about 30 minutes
Total time: about 45 minutes

Calories **67**
Protein **4g.**
Cholesterol **7mg.**
Total fat **2g.**
Saturated fat **1g.**
Sodium **120mg.**

| |
|---|
| 1 tsp. safflower oil |
| 1½ lb. fresh green beans, trimmed and cut into 1-inch pieces |
| 2 tbsp. finely chopped garlic |
| 1 tbsp. grated lemon zest |
| 1½ cups unsalted chicken stock (recipe, page 138) |
| 2 oz. Canadian bacon or lean ham, finely chopped |
| freshly ground black pepper |
| 1 large ripe tomato, cored and cut into wedges |

Heat the oil in a large, nonstick skillet over medium heat. Add the green beans, garlic and lemon zest, and cook them for one minute. Pour in the chicken stock, bring the liquid to a boil, and cook the mixture, stirring frequently, until most of the stock has evaporated and the beans are tender — about five minutes.

Remove the skillet from the heat and stir in the Canadian bacon or ham and some pepper. Transfer the beans to a serving plate and let them cool. Arrange the tomato wedges around the beans. Serve the dish at room temperature or chilled.

# Orange-Walnut Coffeecake

Serves 8
Working time: about 30 minutes
Total time: about 1 hour

Calories **230**
Protein **3g.**
Cholesterol **0mg.**
Total fat **9g.**
Saturated fat **0g.**
Sodium **168mg.**

| |
|---|
| 1 cup fresh orange juice |
| ½ cup dark brown sugar |
| ¼ cup safflower oil |
| grated zest of 2 oranges |
| 1¼ cups cake flour |
| 1 tsp. baking powder |
| 1 tsp. baking soda |
| ¾ cup rolled oats |
| 1 egg white |
| **Streusel topping** |
| ½ tsp. cinnamon |
| 1 tsp. pure vanilla extract |
| 2 tbsp. chopped walnuts |
| 2 tbsp. rolled oats |

Preheat the oven to 350° F. Lightly butter a 9-by-4-inch loaf pan.

Combine the orange juice, brown sugar, oil and orange zest in a large saucepan and bring the mixture to a boil, stirring constantly. Remove the pan from the heat and let the syrup cool while you prepare the remaining ingredients.

Combine the streusel ingredients in a small bowl; set the bowl aside. Sift the cake flour, baking powder ▶

and baking soda together into a bowl. Put the rolled oats in a food processor or a blender and process them into a powder — about 30 seconds. Stir the ground oats into the flour mixture.

When the orange-juice syrup is cool, whisk in the egg white. Stir in the flour mixture until the ingredients are just blended; do not overmix. Pour half of the batter into the prepared pan and then sprinkle half of the streusel mixture over the batter. Pour the remaining batter into the pan and sprinkle the remaining streusel over the top.

Bake the coffeecake until a cake tester inserted into the center comes out clean — 25 to 30 minutes. Let the cake cool in the pan for 15 minutes, then turn it out onto a rack to cool completely before slicing it. Serve the cake slices topped with Fresh Peach Compote.

## Fresh Peach Compote

Serves 8
Working time: about 20 minutes
Total time: about 1 hour and 20 minutes
(includes chilling)

Calories **64**
Protein **1g.**
Cholesterol **0mg.**
Total fat **0g.**
Saturated fat **0g.**
Sodium **0mg.**

| |
|---|
| 1½ lb. ripe peaches, peeled, pitted and thinly sliced |
| 3 tbsp. sugar |
| 3 tbsp. Cointreau or other orange-flavored liqueur |
| 6 tbsp. fresh orange juice |

Combine the sugar, liqueur and orange juice in a small saucepan. Bring the mixture to a boil over medium heat and cook it for one minute. Put the peaches into a bowl, pour in the syrup, and stir well. Refrigerate the compote until it is well chilled — about one hour.

## Raspberry Iced Tea

Serves 8
Working time: about 20 minutes
Total time: about 1 hour and 20 minutes
(includes chilling)

Calories **45**
Protein **1g.**
Cholesterol **0mg.**
Total fat **0g.**
Saturated fat **0g**
Sodium **1mg.**

| |
|---|
| 1½ to 2 cups fresh or frozen raspberries |
| zest and juice of 1 orange |
| 3 tbsp. honey |
| 2 jasmine tea bags, or 1½ tbsp. loose jasmine tea |
| 1 lemon, cut into 8 slices, for garnish |

If you are using frozen raspberries, thaw them. Purée the raspberries in a blender or food processor, then use a wooden spoon to rub the purée through a fine sieve set over a bowl.

Put the orange zest, orange juice, honey and 6 cups of water into a saucepan. Bring the liquid to a boil and add the tea. Remove the saucepan from the heat and let the tea steep for three minutes. Strain the tea into the purée, stir the mixture, then chill it.

Serve the drink garnished with the lemon slices.

**SCANDINAVIAN BRUNCH**

*Chilled Berry Soup*
*Mackerel and Red Potato Salad*
*Grated Beet and Red Cabbage Salad*
*Cucumber Salad with Creamy Green Sauce*
*Curried Potato Lefse*
*Half-Moon Spice Cookies*

Most of the dishes can be prepared ahead. Chill the potatoes for the lefse dough. Make the cookie dough and the berry soup. Prepare the cabbage-and-beet salad and the mackerel salad; salt the cucumbers for the cucumber salad. Bake the cookies and place them in an airtight container. Refrigerate everything else overnight, covered. Make the lefse and store them in the refrigerator or freezer *(editor's note, page 90)*.

Just before the brunch, make the green sauce, decorate the fish salad, and heat the lefse.

# Chilled Berry Soup

Serves 8
Working time: about 30 minutes
Total time: about 2 hours and 30 minutes
(includes chilling)

Calories **139**
Protein **2g.**
Cholesterol **1mg.**
Total fat **1g.**
Saturated fat **0g.**
Sodium **39mg.**

| |
|---|
| 4 cups fresh or frozen raspberries, thawed |
| 4 cups fresh or frozen blueberries, thawed |
| 1 cup dry sherry |
| 1 cup cranberry juice |
| 2 tsp. cider vinegar, raspberry vinegar or blueberry vinegar |
| 2 tbsp. sugar |
| 1 cup buttermilk |

Set aside 24 raspberries to use as a garnish for the soup. Put the remaining raspberries, the blueberries, sherry, cranberry juice, vinegar and sugar into a nonreactive saucepan and bring the mixture to a boil. Reduce the heat and simmer the mixture for five minutes.

Purée the soup in three or four batches in a blender or a food processor. After each batch is puréed, strain it through a fine sieve into a bowl. Cover the soup with plastic wrap and refrigerate it for at least two hours.

To serve, divide the soup among eight bowls and garnish each serving with three of the reserved raspberries and some of the buttermilk. Pass the remaining buttermilk separately in a pitcher for each diner to add to the soup as desired.

*Cool Scandinavian flavors of three salads — beet and cabbage, sliced cucumber, and creamy mackerel and potato — accompany a curry-flavored potato bread called lefse, served with yogurt cheese. A buttermilk-topped berry soup and spice cookies round out the meal.*

# Curried Potato Lefse

Makes 16 lefse
Working time: about 1 hour and 30 minutes
Total time: about 5 hours and 45 minutes
(includes chilling)

| Per lefse: | |
|---|---|
| Calories **130** | 4 medium russet or other baking potatoes (about 2 lb.), peeled and quartered |
| Protein **2g.** | ¼ cup safflower oil |
| Cholesterol **0mg.** | ¼ cup skim milk |
| Total fat **3g.** | 1 tsp. curry powder |
| Saturated fat **0g.** | 2¼ cups unbleached all-purpose flour |
| Sodium **4mg.** | |

Bring 2 quarts of water to a boil in a large saucepan. Add the potatoes, then reduce the heat, and simmer them until they are tender — about 10 minutes. Drain the potatoes thoroughly. Work the potatoes through a food mill, a sieve or a ricer set over a bowl. Allow the potatoes to cool to room temperature, then cover the bowl with plastic wrap, and refrigerate the potatoes until they are very cold — at least four hours.

Add the oil, milk and curry powder to the cold potatoes. Stir the mixture until it is smooth. Add the flour, about ½ cup at a time, kneading the mixture against the sides of the bowl with the heel of your hand after each addition. The dough should be firm but not dry.

Divide the dough into 16 pieces. Preheat an electric skillet to 400° F. or heat a large, nonstick skillet *(box, page 55)* over medium-high heat.

Lightly flour a work surface; use only enough flour to prevent sticking — too much will make the lefse brittle. Use a rolling pin to roll one piece of the dough into a round no more than ⅛ inch thick; the lefse should be as thin as possible. Roll out the remaining pieces of dough in the same manner, stacking the rounds one on top of the other.

Put one of the rounds on the preheated skillet and cook it until the underside is flecked with brown speckles — about one minute. Turn the lefse over and brown the other side.

Transfer the cooked lefse to a clean kitchen towel or cloth spread flat on a work surface and fold the lefse into quarters. Cover the folded lefse with another towel or cloth. Continue to cook the remaining rounds in the same manner, folding and covering each lefse as it is cooked. When the lefse have cooled to room temperature, remove them from the towels and wrap them tightly in plastic wrap until you are ready to serve.

Serve the lefse with the Dill-and-Chive Spread *(recipe, page 51).*

EDITOR'S NOTE: *The lefse can be prepared a day in advance and refrigerated: Divide the folded lefse into groups of four and wrap them in aluminum foil. Reheat the wrapped lefse in a preheated 200° F. oven for about 10 minutes. The wrapped lefse can also be kept in the freezer for up to one month; thaw them and reheat them as described.*

# Mackerel and Red Potato Salad

Serves 8
Working time: about 1 hour and 15 minutes
Total time: about 3 hours and 15 minutes
(includes chilling)

| | |
|---|---|
| Calories **169** | 1 lb. mackerel or trout fillets, skinned and cut into 1-inch pieces |
| Protein **11g.** | ¾ lb. red potatoes, scrubbed and cut into ½-inch cubes |
| Cholesterol **42mg.** | 1 red apple, cored and chopped |
| Total fat **7g.** | 1 small onion, thinly sliced |
| Saturated fat **2g.** | 2 tsp. capers, rinsed and chopped |
| Sodium **167mg.** | 6 tbsp. cider vinegar |
| | 2 tsp. safflower oil |
| | 1 tbsp. sugar |
| | freshly ground black pepper |
| | ¼ cup plain low-fat yogurt |
| | ¼ cup sliced radishes |
| | 1 carrot, thinly sliced |
| | ¼ cup chopped fresh parsley |
| | 2 tbsp. finely cut chives |

Pour enough water into a large skillet to fill it 2 inches deep. Bring the water to a simmer, add the pieces of mackerel or trout, and poach them over medium-low heat until the flesh is opaque and firm to the touch — about two minutes. Remove the fish pieces from the water with a slotted spoon and arrange them in a single layer in the bottom of a deep serving dish.

Pour enough water into a large saucepan to fill it about 1 inch deep. Set a vegetable steamer in the pan and put the potatoes into it. Cover the pan and bring the water to a boil. Steam the potatoes until they are tender — about 10 minutes.

In a bowl, toss the potatoes with the apple, onion and capers. Spread the mixture over the mackerel.

Whisk together the vinegar, oil, sugar and some pepper; pour this dressing over the potatoes. Cover the dish and refrigerate it for at least two hours. (The salad can be refrigerated for as long as overnight.)

Just before serving, spread the yogurt in a thin layer over the salad. Arrange the radish slices, carrot slices, parsley and chives on top, and serve.

## Grated Beet and Red Cabbage Salad

Serves 8
Working time: about 30 minutes
Total time: about 1 hour and 40 minutes
(includes chilling)

Calories **29**
Protein **1g.**
Cholesterol **0mg.**
Total fat **0g.**
Saturated fat **0g.**
Sodium **87mg.**

| |
|---|
| ¾ lb. beets, scrubbed and trimmed, 2 inches of stem left on each beet |
| 2 cups thinly sliced red cabbage (about ½ lb.) |
| ¼ cup apple cider or unsweetened apple juice |
| ½ cup cranberry juice |
| ¼ cup cider vinegar |
| ¼ tsp. salt |
| 1 tsp. caraway seeds |

Put the beets into a saucepan with enough water to cover them by 3 inches. Bring the water to a boil over high heat, reduce the heat, and simmer the beets until they are tender — about 20 minutes. Remove the beets from the water and set them aside to cool.

While the beets are cooking, combine the cabbage, cider or apple juice, cranberry juice, vinegar and salt in a nonreactive saucepan. Bring the mixture to a boil over high heat, reduce the heat, and simmer the cabbage for five minutes. Transfer the cabbage mixture to a large bowl.

When the beets are cool enough to handle, peel and grate them, using the grater's coarsest side. Toss the beets with the cabbage and the caraway seeds; refrigerate the salad, covered, for at least one hour.

EDITOR'S NOTE: *If you wish, this salad can be made up to two days in advance.*

## Cucumber Salad with Creamy Green Sauce

Serves 8
Working time: about 30 minutes
Total time: about 7 hours (includes chilling)

Calories **19**
Protein **1g.**
Cholesterol **2mg.**
Total fat **1g.**
Saturated fat **0g.**
Sodium **279mg.**

| |
|---|
| 2 cucumbers, peeled and thinly sliced |
| 1 tsp. salt |
| **Creamy green sauce** |
| 1 bunch watercress, stemmed, washed and dried |
| 1 small scallion, trimmed and coarsely chopped |
| ¼ cup part-skim ricotta cheese |
| 1 tbsp. fresh lemon juice |
| 1 tsp. sugar |

Toss the cucumber slices with the salt in a bowl. Cover the bowl and refrigerate it for at least six hours.

Rinse the cucumber slices in a colander under cold running water. Drain them thoroughly and transfer them to a salad bowl.

To make the green sauce, purée the watercress, scallion, cheese, lemon juice and sugar in a blender or a food processor. Pour the sauce over the cucumber slices and toss to mix them well. Refrigerate the salad for at least 30 minutes before serving.

## Half-Moon Spice Cookies

Makes 24 cookies
Working time: about 30 minutes
Total time: about 1 hour

Per cookie:
Calories **19**
Protein **0g**
Cholesterol **1mg.**
Total fat **1g.**
Saturated fat **0g**
Sodium **6mg.**

| |
|---|
| 2 tbsp. dark corn syrup |
| 1 tbsp. light or dark brown sugar |
| 1 tbsp. unsalted butter, softened |
| ½ cup unbleached all-purpose flour, sifted |
| ¼ tsp. ground cloves |
| ½ tsp. grated lemon zest |
| 1 egg white, beaten |
| 1 tbsp. slivered almonds |

Put the corn syrup, sugar and butter into a small bowl. Using a wooden spoon, cream the ingredients together. Add the flour, cloves and zest, and mix until the dry ingredients are incorporated. Wrap the dough in plastic wrap and refrigerate it for 30 minutes.

Preheat the oven to 400° F. Lightly oil a baking sheet or line it with parchment paper.

Place the chilled dough on a lightly floured surface and roll it out about ⅛ inch thick. Using a cookie cutter with a 2-inch diameter, cut the dough into rounds. Gather the scraps into a ball, then roll out the dough, and cut more rounds; there should be 12 in all. Brush the rounds with egg white, then cut them in half, press an almond sliver onto each half. Transfer the cookies to the cookie sheet. Bake the cookies until they have lightened slightly in color — five to seven minutes. Transfer the cookies to a rack to cool. Store the cooled cookies in an airtight container.

## BRITISH BRUNCH

---

*Leg of Lamb with Tarragon Sauce*
*Lemon Popovers with Black Pepper*
*Pickled Onion Rings*
*Cauliflower and Leeks with Cheddar Cheese*
*Lady's Kisses*
*Marmalade Buttons*

To simplify the preparation of this British brunch, make the pickled onion rings up to three days before you need them. Bake the cookies ahead, but do not fill them. You may store the cookies at room temperature in an airtight container for up to three days; or, if you prefer, freeze them.

On the day of the brunch, fill the cookies. About one hour and 30 minutes before serving the lamb, put it into the oven. When the lamb has 15 minutes left to go, put the popovers into a second oven. Alternatively, finish cooking the lamb, remove it from the oven, wrap it with foil, and then keep it warm while you bake the popovers. Prepare the cauliflower with Cheddar cheese and leeks last so that the ingredients are hot when the dish goes under the broiler.

# Leg of Lamb with Tarragon

Serves 12
Working time: about 20 minutes
Total time: about 1 hour and 40 minutes

Calories **164**
Protein **21g.**
Cholesterol **67mg.**
Total fat **7g.**
Saturated fat **3g.**
Sodium **164mg.**

| |
| --- |
| *1 leg of lamb (about 5½ lb.), trimmed of fat* |
| *½ tsp. salt* |
| *freshly ground black pepper* |
| *1 tsp. dry mustard* |
| *1½ tbsp. unbleached all-purpose flour* |
| *½ cup fresh bread crumbs* |
| *3 tbsp. chopped fresh tarragon, or 1 tbsp. dried tarragon* |
| *2 cups unsalted chicken stock or unsalted beef stock (recipes, page 138)* |
| *1½ tbsp. cornstarch, mixed with 2 tbsp. water* |

Preheat the oven to 425° F.

In a heavy-bottomed pan, roast the leg of lamb for 20 minutes. Season the lamb with ¼ teaspoon of the salt and some pepper, reduce the heat to 350° F., and continue roasting the meat for 40 minutes more.

Meanwhile, in a small bowl, mix the dry mustard and the flour with 1 tablespoon of water to make a paste. In a separate bowl, mix the bread crumbs with 2 tablespoons of the fresh tarragon or 2 teaspoons of the ►

---

*The central feature of this British brunch, a bread-crumb-crusted leg of lamb, is mated with tarragon sauce, pickled onion rings, popovers and cauliflower with Cheddar cheese sauce. For dessert, there are two kinds of cookies, one with marmalade and one with raspberry jam and almonds.*

dried tarragon. Set both bowls aside.

Remove the pan from the oven and increase the oven heat to 425° F. again. Using a pastry brush, paint the top of the lamb with the mustard paste. Sprinkle the bread-crumb mixture over the lamb, pressing it down lightly so that it adheres to the meat. Return the lamb to the oven and continue roasting until the bread crumbs are browned and a meat thermometer inserted into the center of the meat registers 145° F. — about 15 minutes. Transfer the lamb to a serving platter and let it stand for about 20 minutes.

To make the sauce, discard the fat that has collected in the roasting pan, leaving any caramelized juices in the pan. Set the pan on the stove top over medium heat and pour in the stock. Bring the stock to a simmer, scraping up any browned bits with a wooden spoon to dissolve them. Strain the liquid into a small saucepan.

Stir the remaining tablespoon of fresh tarragon or teaspoon of dried tarragon, the remaining ¼ teaspoon of salt and some black pepper into the sauce. Simmer the liquid for three minutes; then stir in the cornstarch mixture. Cook the sauce, stirring constantly, until it thickens. Keep it warm over very low heat. Carve the lamb into thin slices and serve it with the sauce.

# Lemon Popovers with Black Pepper

THIS RECIPE USES HALF THE AMOUNT OF EGG YOLK CALLED FOR IN A TRADITIONAL POPOVER RECIPE.

Makes 12 popovers
Working time: about 10 minutes
Total time: about 1 hour

Per popover:
Calories **120**
Protein **5g.**
Cholesterol **49mg.**
Total fat **3g.**
Saturated fat **1g.**
Sodium **130mg.**

| |
|---|
| 2 eggs, plus 3 egg whites |
| grated zest of 1 lemon |
| ¼ tsp. freshly ground black pepper |
| 1 tbsp. safflower oil |
| 2 cups unbleached all-purpose flour |
| ½ tsp. salt |
| 2 cups low-fat milk |

Preheat the oven to 425° F. Lightly oil a popover pan or a muffin pan.

Put the eggs, egg whites, lemon zest, pepper and oil into a bowl and whisk them together. In another bowl, stir together the flour and the salt, then whisk in the milk. Pour in the egg mixture and whip the batter with a whisk or an electric mixer until it is well blended. Alternatively, you may combine the ingredients in a blender, processing the batter until it is smooth. Pour the batter into the popover pan or muffin pan, filling each cup about half full.

Bake the popovers for 20 minutes. Reduce the heat to 400° F. and bake the popovers until they are well browned — 20 to 30 minutes more. Serve the popovers immediately.

# Pickled Onion Rings

Serves 12
Working time: about 15 minutes
Total time: about one day (includes marinating)

Calories **51**
Protein **1g.**
Cholesterol **0mg.**
Total fat **0g.**
Saturated fat **0g.**
Sodium **3mg.**

| |
|---|
| 2 cups malt vinegar, cider vinegar or distilled white vinegar |
| 1 cup sugar |
| 2 tsp. dill seeds |
| 1 dried hot chili pepper, or ⅛ tsp. hot red-pepper flakes |
| 3 lb. onions, preferably a combination of red and white varieties, thinly sliced (about 8 cups) |

Put the vinegar, sugar, dill seeds and chili pepper or red-pepper flakes into a nonreactive saucepan and bring the mixture to a boil. Reduce the heat and simmer the mixture for three minutes. Put the onion slices into a bowl and separate them into rings. Hold a sieve over the onions and strain the hot vinegar mixture onto them. Stir to coat the onions with the liquid. Cover the bowl and put it into the refrigerator. Allow the onions to marinate for at least 12 hours; stir the mixture occasionally. The onions can be marinated for up to three days if they are kept refrigerated.

Before serving, drain the onions, discarding the liquid. The pickled onions may be served chilled or at room temperature.

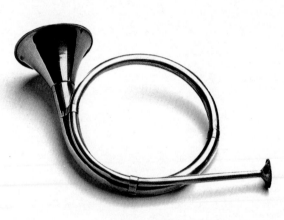

# Cauliflower and Leeks with Cheddar Cheese

Serves 12
Working time: about 15 minutes
Total time: about 40 minutes

Calories **82**
Protein **4g.**
Cholesterol **8mg.**
Total fat **4g.**
Saturated fat **2g.**
Sodium **64mg.**

| |
|---|
| 1 ripe tomato |
| 1 cup unsalted chicken stock (recipe, page 138) |
| 2 leeks, trimmed, split, washed thoroughly to remove all grit and sliced crosswise into ¼-inch-thick pieces |
| 2 heads of cauliflower, trimmed and cut into florets |
| 1 tbsp. safflower oil |

| ¼ cup unbleached all-purpose flour |
| :---: |
| ½ cup skim milk |
| ¾ cup grated sharp Cheddar cheese (about 3 oz.) |
| ⅛ tsp. ground white pepper |

Put the tomato on a cutting surface with its stem end down. With a small, sharp knife, cut wide strips of flesh from the tomato, discarding the seeds and juice. Cut the strips of tomato into julienne and set them aside.

Pour the stock and 1 cup of water into a large saucepan and set a vegetable steamer in the pan. Put the leeks into the bottom of the steamer, then the cauliflower. Cover the pan, bring the liquid to a boil, and steam the vegetables until they are tender — seven to 10 minutes. Transfer the cauliflower and leeks to separate bowls; reserve the steaming liquid.

Heat the oil in a small saucepan over medium heat. Whisk in the flour to form a smooth paste and cook it for two minutes. Add the reserved steaming liquid, whisking constantly to prevent lumps from forming, and bring the mixture to a boil. Pour in the milk and return the liquid to a boil, whisking frequently. Reduce the heat and simmer the sauce for five minutes. Remove the pan from the heat and stir in ½ cup of the cheese and the white pepper.

Preheat the broiler.

Arrange half of the cauliflower florets in a gratin dish. Spread the leeks over the cauliflower in the dish and layer the remaining cauliflower over the leeks. Pour the cheese sauce over the vegetables, arrange the tomato julienne on top, and sprinkle the remaining cheese over all. Broil the dish just until the top starts to brown — about four minutes. Serve the dish at once.

EDITOR'S NOTE: *If you wish to make this dish in advance, put it into a 300° F. oven for 10 minutes to heat the vegetables through before putting it under the broiler.*

## Lady's Kisses

Makes 12 cookies
Working time: about 10 minutes
Total time: about 20 minutes

*Per cookie:*
Calories **98**
Protein **2g.**
Cholesterol **0mg.**
Total fat **4g.**
Saturated fat **0g.**
Sodium **23mg.**

| 2 oz. sliced almonds (about ½ cup) |
| :---: |
| ⅓ cup sugar |
| ⅔ cup unbleached all-purpose flour |
| 2 tbsp. unsalted margarine, preferably corn oil, melted |
| ¼ tsp. pure vanilla extract |
| 2 tbsp. raspberry jam |

Preheat the oven to 425° F. Lightly oil a baking sheet or line it with parchment paper.

Put the almonds and sugar into a food processor and process them, using short bursts of power, until the almonds are finely ground — one minute to one minute and 30 seconds. Sprinkle the flour over the ground almonds and then pour in the margarine and vanilla.

Process the dough in short bursts until it is smooth — about one minute more.

Roll a heaping teaspoon of the dough between your palms to form a ball; place it on the baking sheet. Shape the remaining dough in the same way. Bake the cookies for five minutes. Remove the baking sheet from the oven and press down lightly on the cookies with the bottom of a glass to flatten them. Return the cookies to the oven and bake them until they are lightly browned — about five minutes more.

Transfer the cookies to a rack to cool. Store the cooled cookies in an airtight container. When you are ready to serve the cookies, dab ½ teaspoon of the jam on the center of each one.

## Marmalade Buttons

Makes 12 sandwich cookies
Working time: about 15 minutes
Total time: about 25 minutes

*Per cookie:*
Calories **66**
Protein **1g.**
Cholesterol **0mg.**
Total fat **4g.**
Saturated fat **1g.**
Sodium **44mg.**

| ¼ cup unsalted margarine, preferably corn oil |
| :---: |
| ⅓ cup confectioners' sugar |
| ½ cup unbleached all-purpose flour |
| grated zest of 1 orange |
| 1 tbsp. orange marmalade |

Preheat the oven to 400° F. Lightly oil a baking sheet or line it with parchment paper.

With an electric mixer, whip the margarine until it is fluffy. Gradually add the sugar, flour and orange zest, and beat the dough until it is thoroughly mixed. Divide the dough into 24 pieces and roll one between your palms to form a ball, then place it on the baking sheet. Shape the rest of the dough in the same way.

Bake the cookies for five minutes. Remove the cookies from the oven and press them down slightly with the bottom of a glass to flatten them. Return the cookies to the oven and bake them until they are lightly browned — about five minutes more. Transfer the cookies to a rack to cool.

Store the cooled cookies in an airtight container. When you are ready to serve the cookies, spread about ¼ teaspoon of marmalade on the bottom side of a cookie. Press the bottom side of another cookie onto the marmalade to form a sandwich. Repeat the process with the remaining cookies.

uncovered, until it is very soft and begins to break apart — about one hour.

While the rice is cooking, heat the safflower oil in a small skillet over medium-low heat. Add the garlic and cook it, stirring often, until it is crisp and brown — four to five minutes. Transfer the garlic to a paper towel and let it drain. Put the garlic, ginger, bean sprouts, cilantro and lime wedges into small serving bowls, and set them aside.

About five minutes before serving, stir the sugar, fish sauce or soy sauce, salt and some pepper into the hot soup. Add the beef strips and the scallions, and bring the liquid to a boil. Reduce the heat to medium and simmer the soup until the beef is just cooked — about three minutes.

Ladle the soup into individual bowls. Pass the garnishes separately, inviting the diners to season their own soup with them.

EDITOR'S NOTE: *Canned beef broth or bouillon may be substituted for the brown stock, but if you do use it, be sure to eliminate the salt from the recipe.*

# Fried Chinese Turnip Cakes

Serves 8
Working time: about 20 minutes
Total time: about 1 hour and 20 minutes

Calories **59**
Protein **2g.**
Cholesterol **0mg.**
Total fat **1g.**
Saturated fat **0g.**
Sodium **91mg.**

| |
|---|
| 1½ lb. Chinese turnip, or white turnip, or daikon radish, peeled and coarsely grated |
| ½ cup unsalted chicken stock (recipe, page 138) |
| ¾ cup cake flour |
| ½ oz. dried shrimp, finely chopped (about ¼ cup) |
| ½ red or green pepper, seeded, deribbed and finely diced |
| 2 egg whites, lightly beaten |
| 2 tsp. rice vinegar or distilled white vinegar |
| ¼ tsp. salt |
| freshly ground black pepper |
| 2 tsp. safflower oil |

Pour enough water into a large saucepan to fill it about 1 inch deep. Set a vegetable steamer in the pan and bring the water to a boil. Put the turnip into the steamer, cover the pot, and reduce the heat to medium low. Steam the turnip until it is very tender — about 15 minutes. While the turnip is cooking, blend the chicken stock and flour in a 2-quart saucepan to form a smooth paste.

Drain the turnip in a sieve, pressing it with the back of a wooden spoon to get rid of any excess water. Add the turnip to the flour paste and cook the mixture over low heat, stirring constantly, for three minutes.

Remove the pan from the heat and stir in the dried shrimp, red or green pepper, egg whites, vinegar, salt, and one or two grindings of black pepper. Spoon the mixture into a lightly oiled 4-by-8-inch glass or enameled loaf pan, smooth the top with the back of a ▶

## CHINESE BRUNCH

*Rice Congee*
*Fried Chinese Turnip Cakes*
*Beef Pot Stickers with Soy Dipping Sauce*
*Steamed Buns Filled with Sweet Red Bean Paste*
*Almond Milk with Apricots*

Simplify the preparation of this brunch by making the congee, buns, almond jelly and the sauce for the pot stickers the day before; refrigerate them overnight. Cook the mixture for the turnip cakes in advance and leave it in the loaf pan. Form the pot stickers and cover them with a damp towel and plastic wrap. Put the steamed buns into an airtight bag.

On the day of the brunch, reheat the congee and prepare its garnishes; if the congee has thickened, add a little stock or water to thin it. Cook the pot stickers and, while they simmer, slice and fry the turnip cakes. The buns need only to be steamed briefly to reheat them. To serve the jelly, simply cut it into squares.

# Rice Congee

CONGEE IS A CHINESE PORRIDGE THAT CAN BE FLAVORED WITH A VARIETY OF INGREDIENTS, BOTH SWEET AND SAVORY.

Serves 8
Working time: about 30 minutes
Total time: about 1 hour

Calories **167**
Protein **10g.**
Cholesterol **21mg.**
Total fat **1g.**
Saturated fat **0g.**
Sodium **132mg.**

| |
|---|
| ¾ cup long-grain rice |
| 4 cups unsalted brown stock or unsalted chicken stock (recipes, page 138) |
| 1 tbsp. safflower oil |
| 6 garlic cloves, finely chopped |
| ¼ cup julienned fresh ginger (about 2 oz.) |
| ¼ lb. bean sprouts |
| 1 cup cilantro leaves |
| 1 lime, cut into 16 wedges |
| 2 tbsp. sugar |
| 1 tsp. fish sauce or low-sodium soy sauce |
| 1 tsp. salt |
| freshly ground black pepper |
| ½ lb. beef tenderloin, trimmed of fat and cut into thin strips |
| 3 scallions, trimmed and cut into ½-inch lengths |

Put the rice, stock and 4 cups of water into a large saucepan; bring the liquid to a boil. Stir the mixture, then reduce the heat to medium, and simmer the rice,

*This Chinese brunch begins with a bowl of rice soup, called congee, and, on the tray, a selection of garnishes. Beef pot stickers with soy dipping sauce, steamed buns filled with bean paste, and fried turnip cakes follow. Squares of almond milk jelly provide the refreshing dessert.*

spoon, and cover the pan tightly with plastic wrap.

Place the loaf pan in a pot large enough to hold it and pour in ½ inch of water. Bring the water to a boil. Cover the pot, reduce the heat to medium low, and poach the loaf until it is firm to the touch — about 40 minutes. Remove the loaf pan from the pot and allow the loaf to cool completely. If you wish, it may be chilled overnight.

Loosen the loaf from the sides of the pan with a knife, then turn it out onto a cutting board. Cut the loaf into ¼-inch slices.

Brush a large, nonstick skillet with 1 teaspoon of the oil, then set the skillet over medium-high heat. Add half of the turnip cake slices and sauté them, turning them once, until they are brown on both sides. Transfer the slices to a heated platter. Brush the skillet with the remaining teaspoon of oil and brown the remaining slices in the same manner.

EDITOR'S NOTE: *Dried shrimp are available in Asian markets.*

# Beef Pot Stickers with Soy Dipping Sauce

Serves 8
Working time: about 1 hour
Total time: about 1 hour and 30 minutes

Calories **62**
Protein **7g.**
Cholesterol **7mg.**
Total fat **1g.**
Saturated fat **0g.**
Sodium **132mg.**

| |
|---|
| ½ lb. Nappa cabbage or green cabbage, cut into fine shreds |
| ¼ lb. ground beef round |
| ¼ cup peeled, chopped fresh water chestnuts (about 5), or ¼ cup rinsed, drained, chopped canned water chestnuts |
| 1 scallion, trimmed and finely chopped |
| 1 tbsp. rice wine or dry sherry |
| 1 tsp. low-sodium soy sauce |
| ⅛ tsp. white pepper |
| 1 tsp. cornstarch |
| 24 wonton wrappers, trimmed into circles, or 24 gyoza wrappers (plus 2 or 3 extra wrappers to use if others tear) |
| 1 tsp. safflower oil |
| **Soy dipping sauce** |
| ½ cup unsalted chicken stock or unsalted brown stock (recipes, page 138) |
| 3 tbsp. rice vinegar or distilled white vinegar |
| 1 tbsp. low-sodium soy sauce |
| 1 tbsp. trimmed, julienned scallions |
| 1 tbsp. finely julienned carrot |
| 1 tsp. sugar |

Put all of the ingredients for the soy dipping sauce into a small, decorative bowl and stir them until the sugar is dissolved. Set the bowl aside.

Put the shredded cabbage into a colander and set it in the sink or over a large bowl. Pour 3 or 4 cups of boiling water over the cabbage to blanch it. Press out any excess water with the back of a wooden spoon.

To prepare the filling, put the beef into a large bowl

and add the blanched cabbage, water chestnuts, scallion, wine, soy sauce, pepper and cornstarch. Stir the contents of the bowl thoroughly.

To make the dumplings, place a heaping teaspoonful of the filling on a wrapper, slightly off center. Fold the circle into a crescent-shaped dumpling *(technique, page 124)*. Repeat the process with the remaining wrappers, covering the dumplings with a slightly damp cloth as they are completed. (The dumplings can be made ahead of time and kept in the refrigerator, covered, on a lightly floured tray.)

Brush the safflower oil onto the surface of a non-stick skillet and set the pan over medium-high heat. When the skillet is hot, arrange as many of the dumplings as will fit in a single layer in the pan without touching one another; the sealed sides should face up. Reduce the heat to medium and cook the dumplings until they turn golden brown on the bottom. Add enough cold water to come halfway up the sides of the dumplings. Partially cover the skillet and simmer the dumplings until almost all of the liquid has evaporated or been absorbed by the dumplings — about 10 minutes. Transfer the dumplings to a serving dish and keep them warm while you cook the remaining dumplings. Serve the dumplings with the soy dipping sauce.

EDITOR'S NOTE: *Wonton and gyoza wrappers are available in Asian markets and in some supermarkets.*

# Steamed Buns Filled with Sweet Red Bean Paste

THESE BUNS CAN BE PREPARED A DAY IN ADVANCE AND REFRIGERATED, THEN STEAMED FOR ABOUT FIVE MINUTES TO REHEAT THEM.

Serves 8
Working time: about 50 minutes
Total time: about 4 hours (includes soaking and cooking time for the beans)

Calories **243**
Protein **8g.**
Cholesterol **0mg.**
Total fat **4g.**
Saturated fat **0g.**
Sodium **3mg.**

| |
|---|
| 1 package fast-rising dry yeast (about 1 tbsp.) |
| 2 tsp. sugar |
| 1¾ cups unbleached all-purpose flour, sifted |
| 2 tbsp. safflower oil |
| **Sweet red bean paste** |
| 1¼ cups kidney beans, picked over |
| ⅓ cup sugar |
| 1 tsp. pure vanilla extract |
| 1 tsp. beet juice (optional) |

To prepare the bean paste, rinse the beans and then place them in a small saucepan with enough water to cover them. Discard any beans that float to the surface. Cover the saucepan, leaving the lid ajar, and slowly bring the liquid to a boil over medium-low heat. Boil the beans for two minutes, then turn off the heat and soak the beans, covered, for at least one hour.

After the beans have finished soaking, drain them and return them to the pot. Pour in 3 cups of water and bring the beans to a boil. Reduce the heat and simmer them until they begin to split and are very tender — about one hour and 30 minutes. Drain the beans, reserving ¼ cup of their cooking liquid. Put the beans in a food processor or a blender. Add the sugar, the vanilla extract and the reserved cooking liquid, and purée the mixture.

Transfer the puréed beans to a sieve and, holding it over a small saucepan, force the mixture through the sieve with the back of a spoon. Cook the mixture over low heat, stirring frequently, until all of the excess liquid has evaporated — about five minutes. Transfer the bean paste to a bowl, then cover the bowl, and refrigerate the filling until you are ready to fill the buns.

To make the buns, combine the yeast, sugar and flour in a large mixing bowl. Heat ½ cup of water and the oil in a saucepan just until they are hot to the touch (130° F.). Stir the hot liquid into the flour mixture with a wooden spoon to combine the ingredients thoroughly. Turn the dough out onto a floured work surface. Knead the dough, adding a few tablespoons of flour if it is too sticky, until the dough is smooth and elastic — four to five minutes. Transfer the dough to a lightly oiled bowl, turn it once to coat it with the oil, and cover the bowl with a damp towel or plastic wrap. Place the bowl in a warm, draft-free place and let the dough double in bulk — about 30 minutes.

When the dough has risen, punch it down and then transfer it to a floured work surface. Divide the dough into four pieces; cover three of the pieces with a towel. Roll out one piece of dough into a ¼-inch-thick rectangle measuring about 10 inches by 7 inches.

With a 3-inch-wide cookie cutter, cut out six rounds from the rectangle. Place a half tablespoon of the bean-paste filling in the center of one round and then gently gather up the edge of the dough around the bean paste; pinch the edge together and twist it closed to form a bun (technique, page 124). Repeat the procedure for the remaining five rounds.

Line two tiers of a bamboo steamer with perforated wax paper. Place the buns, sealed side down, on the paper — about 12 per tier.

Roll out a second piece of dough. Cut out six more rounds and fill them as described above. Position the six new buns on the tray. Continue shaping and filling the remaining dough until you have 24 buns. Cover the steamer tray and place it in a warm, draft-free place for 20 minutes.

To steam the buns, set the covered steamer tray in a wok or a pot filled with 1 inch of boiling water. Steam the buns until they are firm yet still springy to the touch — about 20 minutes.

Remove the buns from the steamer and, if you like, paint a decorative design on their tops using a small artist's brush dipped in a little beet juice.

The buns can be served immediately, or they can be stored in a sealed plastic bag in the refrigerator for a day. Reheat the buns by steaming them, as described above, for five to seven minutes.

EDITOR'S NOTE: *If you do not have a bamboo steamer, you may use a vegetable steamer. Pour enough water into a pot to fill it 1 inch deep and set the vegetable steamer in the pot. Cut out 24 small rounds of wax paper and place the buns on the rounds. Arrange as many of the buns as will fit in the steamer without touching each other. Cover the pot and steam the buns as directed in the recipe; repeat the process as many times as necessary to steam the remaining buns. Alternatively, you may set a plate on a bowl in the pot to steam the buns.*

## Almond Milk with Apricots

Serves 8
Working time: about 10 minutes
Total time: about 2 hours and 10 minutes
(includes chilling)

Calories **77**
Protein **4g.**
Cholesterol **4mg.**
Total fat **1g.**
Saturated fat **1g.**
Sodium **30mg.**

| |
|---|
| 7½ tsp. unflavored powdered gelatin (3 envelopes) |
| 1½ cups low-fat milk |
| ⅓ cup sugar |
| 1 tbsp. pure almond extract |
| 8 canned apricot halves, drained, rinsed if packed in syrup, and patted dry |
| 1 tbsp. sliced almonds (optional) |
| 1 tbsp. toasted coconut (optional) |

Pour ½ cup of cold water into a bowl and sprinkle the gelatin onto the water. While the gelatin softens, bring 1 cup of water to a boil, then pour it into the bowl, stirring to dissolve the gelatin. Add the milk, sugar and almond extract, and stir to dissolve the sugar. Pour the mixture into an 8-inch-square pan, and distribute the apricot halves in the mixture so that when the dessert is cut into squares each will contain an apricot half. Refrigerate the dessert until it is set — about two hours; the dessert may be kept in the refrigerator overnight.

To serve, cut the dessert into squares, place the squares on a serving platter and, if you like, top each with some of the almonds and coconut.

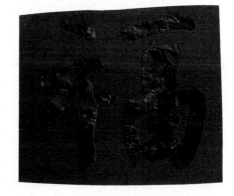

**SOUTHWEST BRUNCH**
—

*Cornmeal Griddlecakes*
*Marinated Grilled Pork Loin with Orange Sauce*
*Salsa Verde*
*Individual Molded Tomato Salads*
*Strawberry and Grapefruit Salad*
*Pink Lime Freeze*

The salsa verde and the tomato salads for this brunch can be prepared a day ahead. If you like, the meat can be sliced and the marinade prepared . Freeze the mixture for the lime drink. Refrigerate everything else.

On the day of the brunch, get the pork into its marinade. Make the strawberry-and-grapefruit salad and chill it. Shred the lettuce for the tomato salads, then unmold them onto the lettuce. Transfer the pink lime freeze to the refrigerator to soften for about 45 minutes before processing it. About half an hour before serving time, make the griddlecakes. Keep the griddlecakes warm while you grill the pork.

# Cornmeal Griddlecakes

Makes twelve 4-inch cakes
Working (and total) time: about 30 minutes

Calories **111**
Protein **4g.**
Cholesterol **47mg.**
Total fat **2g.**
Saturated fat **1g.**
Sodium **113mg.**

| |
|---|
| 1 cup cornmeal |
| 1 tsp. sugar |
| ¼ tsp. salt |
| ½ cup low-fat milk |
| 1 egg, lightly beaten |

Combine the cornmeal, sugar and salt in a bowl. Pour in 1 cup of boiling water all at once and stir until the ingredients are well blended. Let the mixture stand for two minutes.

In a small bowl, whisk together the milk and egg. Pour this mixture into the bowl containing the cornmeal mixture and stir the batter until it is smooth.

Heat a large, nonstick griddle or skillet *(box, page 55)* over medium-high heat until a few drops of cold water dance when sprinkled on the surface. Drop the batter, 2 tablespoons at.a time, onto the hot surface, then use the back of the spoon to spread the batter into 4-inch rounds. Cook the griddlecakes until the surface of each is covered with bubbles and the underside is browned — about two minutes. Turn the cakes over and cook them until the other sides are browned ▶

*Golden cornmeal griddlecakes are served with grilled pork loin and a bowl of zesty salsa verde. Tomato salads on lettuce and a tomato-lime beverage accompany the meal. For dessert, strawberries are paired with grapefruit segments.*

— about one minute more.

Transfer the griddlecakes to a serving plate and keep them warm while you cook the remaining batter. Serve the griddlecakes warm.

## Marinated Grilled Pork Loin with Orange Sauce

Serves 6
Working time: about 20 minutes
Total time: about one hour and 10 minutes
(includes marinating)

Calories **107**
Protein **12g.**
Cholesterol **37mg.**
Total fat **4g.**
Saturated fat **1g.**
Sodium **30mg.**

| |
|---|
| ¼ cup frozen orange-juice concentrate, thawed |
| ¼ cup malt vinegar |
| 2 garlic cloves, finely chopped |
| freshly ground black pepper |
| 14 oz. pork loin, trimmed of fat and cut into 18 thin slices |

Mix together the orange-juice concentrate, vinegar, garlic and some pepper in a large, shallow dish. Lay the slices of pork in the marinade, turning them over to coat them. Cover the dish and marinate the pork at room temperature for one hour or in the refrigerator for three hours.

If you plan to grill the pork, light the coals about 30 minutes before cooking time; to broil, preheat the broiler for 10 minutes.

Remove the pork from the marinade. Transfer the marinade to a small saucepan and simmer it over medium-low heat until it has thickened slightly — about three minutes. Set the sauce aside.

Grill or broil the pork slices until they are browned and no longer pink inside — about one minute on each side. Arrange the pork slices on a warmed serving platter. Briefly reheat the sauce and pour it over the meat. Serve at once.

## Salsa Verde

Makes about 1½ cups
Working time: about 20 minutes
Total time: about 1 hour and 20 minutes
(includes chilling)

Per 4 tablespoons:
Calories **16**
Protein **0g.**
Cholesterol **0mg.**
Total fat **0g.**
Saturated fat **0g.**
Sodium **4mg.**

| |
|---|
| ½ lb. tomatillos, husked, cored and finely chopped, or ½ lb. green tomatoes, seeded and finely chopped |
| 1 jalapeño pepper, seeded, deribbed and finely chopped (caution, page 103) |
| 3 garlic cloves, finely chopped |
| 1 small onion, finely chopped |
| ¼ cup fresh lime juice |
| 1 tbsp. chopped cilantro |

In a small bowl stir together all of the ingredients. Cover the bowl with plastic wrap and refrigerate the salsa verde until it is cold — about one hour. Serve the salsa with the griddlecakes and the grilled pork.

## Individual Molded Tomato Salads

Serves 6
Working time: about 1 hour
Total time: about 3 hours (includes chilling)

Calories **44**
Protein **3g.**
Cholesterol **0mg.**
Total fat **0g.**
Saturated fat **0g.**
Sodium **111mg.**

| |
|---|
| 14 oz. canned unsalted whole tomatoes, with their juice |
| 1 tbsp. unflavored powdered gelatin |
| ½ cup fresh or frozen peas |
| 2 sweet red peppers, seeded, deribbed and finely chopped |
| 3 scallions, trimmed and finely chopped |
| ½ cucumber, peeled, seeded and finely chopped |
| 1 celery stalk, trimmed and finely chopped |
| 2 tbsp. fresh lemon juice |
| 1 tsp. sugar |
| ½ tsp. hot red-pepper sauce |
| ¼ tsp. salt |
| 2 cups shredded lettuce |

Purée the tomatoes and their juice in a blender or food processor. Strain the purée and discard the seeds. Pour 1¼ cups of the purée into a large bowl.

Pour ½ cup of the remaining purée into a small saucepan; reserve any remaining purée for another use. Sprinkle the gelatin over the purée in the saucepan; let the gelatin stand until it is spongy — about five minutes. Place the pan over low heat and bring the purée to a simmer, whisking to dissolve the gelatin. Remove the mixture from the heat and set it aside.

If you are using fresh peas, cook them in boiling water until they are tender — about three minutes; frozen peas need only be thawed. Add the peas, peppers, scallions, cucumber, celery, lemon juice, sugar, hot red-pepper sauce and salt to the purée in the bowl.

Pour the gelatin mixture into the bowl with the vegetables and stir well. Divide the tomato salad among six ¾-cup ramekins. Refrigerate the ramekins until the tomato salad has set — at least two hours.

To serve, line six plates with the lettuce. Dip the bottoms of the ramekins in hot water, then invert the ramekins onto the lettuce and lift them from the salads.

EDITOR'S NOTE: *The salads can be unmolded two hours in advance and kept in the refrigerator, covered with plastic wrap, until serving time. This recipe can also be used to fill a single 4½-cup mold.*

# Strawberry and Grapefruit Salad

Serves 6
Working time: about 30 minutes
Total time: about 1 hour and 30 minutes
(includes chilling)

Calories **93**
Protein **1g.**
Cholesterol **0mg.**
Total fat **0g.**
Saturated fat **0g.**
Sodium **1mg.**

| |
| --- |
| *4 grapefruits* |
| *2 pints strawberries, hulled, halved if large* |
| *3 tbsp. Triple Sec or other orange-flavored liqueur* |
| *¼ cup sugar* |
| *mint sprigs for garnish (optional)* |

Use a sharp knife to slice off both ends of one of the grapefruits so the flesh just shows through. With the grapefruit standing on a flat end, cut around the flesh, following the contour of the fruit, to remove vertical strips of the peel and pith *(technique, page 25)*. Working over a bowl to catch the juice, hold the peeled grapefruit in one hand and carefully slice between the flesh and membrane to free each segment; let the segments fall into the bowl. Remove the pits from the segments and discard them. Squeeze any remaining juice from the membrane into the bowl. Repeat these steps with the remaining grapefruits.

Put the strawberries, liqueur and sugar into the bowl with the grapefruit segments and juice; toss the fruit gently with a wooden spoon. Cover the fruit and chill it thoroughly — at least one hour. Serve the salad in chilled bowls, garnished with mint sprigs if you like.

### Chilies — A Cautionary Note

Both dried and fresh hot chilies should be handled with care. Their flesh and seeds contain volatile oils that can make skin tingle and cause eyes to burn. Rubber gloves offer protection — but the cook should still be careful not to touch the face, lips or eyes when working with chilies.

Soaking fresh chilies in cold, salted water for an hour will remove some of their fire. If canned chilies are substituted for fresh ones, they should be rinsed in cold water in order to eliminate as much of the brine used to preserve them as possible.

# Pink Lime Freeze

Makes 6 servings
Working time: about 15 minutes
Total time: about 2 hours and 15 minutes
(includes freezing)

Calories **76**
Protein **0g.**
Cholesterol **0mg.**
Total fat **0g.**
Saturated fat **0g.**
Sodium **2mg.**

| |
| --- |
| *½ cup sugar* |
| *¾ cup fresh lime juice* |
| *1 ripe tomato, peeled, seeded and puréed, or ½ cup low-sodium tomato juice* |
| *6 thin lime slices for garnish* |

Pour 1 cup of water into a saucepan and stir in the sugar. Bring the mixture to a boil, reduce the heat, and simmer the sugar syrup for two minutes. Transfer the syrup to a shallow pan and stir in 3 cups of cold water, the lime juice and the tomato purée. Freeze the liquid for at least two hours, stirring it every half hour.

Just before serving, break the frozen mixture into chunks and process them in two batches in a blender until the mixture is smooth but slushy. Pour the drink into six chilled glasses and garnish each one with a slice of lime.

## WINTER BRUNCH

*Grouper Stuffed with Pickled Vegetables*
*Broccoli Salad with Hot Red-Pepper Vinaigrette*
*Navy Bean and Potato Salad with Onions and Sage*
*Fennel Toast*
*Fresh Fruit Winter Salad*
*Cardamom-and-Ginger Coffee*

A great deal of the work for this winter brunch menu can be done the day before the brunch. Soak the beans and prepare the saged onions for the navy bean and potato salad. Make the pickled vegetables for the fish stuffing, the fennel-onion mixture for the toast, and the fruit salad. Cut the broccoli and make the hot red-pepper vinaigrette for the broccoli salad. Cover everything and store it in the refrigerator.

On the day of the brunch, cook the beans, onions and potatoes for the bean salad. Stuff the fish with the pickled vegetables and then bake the assembly. Partially cook the broccoli and, when it is cool, toss it with the hot red-pepper vinaigrette. Slice the bread, spread on the fennel-onion mixture, and bake the slices until they are toasted.

a small saucepan and bring the liquid to a boil. Immediately pour the boiling liquid over the vegetables and toss the mixture well. Squeeze the vegetables firmly, toss them again, and then set them aside to marinate for about 20 minutes. Toss the vegetables again and squeeze them firmly to extract the excess liquid and discard it.

Preheat the oven to 325° F. In a small saucepan, warm the butter, oil, lemon juice, salt and pepper over low heat until the butter has melted. Brush a shallow baking dish large enough to accommodate the fish with some of the lemon butter. Place one of the fillets, skinned side down, in the dish. Brush some of the lemon butter over the fillet and then cover it evenly with the vegetables. Place the second fillet on the work surface skinned side up; brush the fillet with half of the remaining lemon butter. Place the fillet, buttered side down, on top of the vegetables. Brush the remaining lemon butter over the top and sides of the assembly. Bake the fish for 45 minutes.

In the meantime, prepare the carrot garnish. Thinly slice the 2 remaining carrots on the diagonal. Bring 2 cups of water to a boil in a small saucepan. Add the carrots and cook them just until they are tender — four to five minutes. Drain the carrots, refresh them under cold running water and set them aside.

When the fish is ready, remove it from the oven and let it stand while you bake the fennel toast. Garnish the stuffed fish with the carrot slices, arranging them in two rows down the center.

# Grouper Stuffed with Pickled Vegetables

Serves 8
Working time: about 40 minutes
Total time: about 1 hour and 45 minutes

Calories **185**
Protein **25g.**
Cholesterol **49mg.**
Total fat **4g.**
Saturated fat **1g.**
Sodium **216mg.**

| |
|---|
| 6 carrots |
| ½ small green cabbage, cored and very thinly sliced (about 6 cups) |
| 1 onion, very thinly sliced |
| ½ cup cider vinegar |
| 1 tbsp. sugar |
| 1 tbsp. unsalted butter |
| 1 tbsp. safflower oil |
| 1½ tbsp. fresh lemon juice |
| ¼ tsp. salt |
| freshly ground black pepper |
| one 5-lb. grouper or tilefish, filleted and skinned |

To make the pickled vegetables, grate 4 of the carrots and put them, along with the cabbage and onion, into a large bowl. Combine the vinegar and sugar in

*Carrot slices decorate a baked grouper stuffed with pickled vegetables and served with fennel toast, broccoli with a red-pepper vinaigrette, and a hearty bean and potato salad. And, for a light, refreshing close — a mug of spiced coffee and a salad of winter fruits.*

# Broccoli Salad with Hot Red-Pepper Vinaigrette

Serves 8
Working (and total) time: about 30 minutes

Calories **37**
Protein **2g.**
Cholesterol **0mg.**
Total fat **2g.**
Saturated fat **0g.**
Sodium **52mg.**

| |
|---|
| 1⅛ tsp. salt |
| 1½ lb. broccoli, the florets separated from the stems, the stems peeled and sliced on the diagonal into ⅛-inch-thick ovals |
| 1 tbsp. fresh lemon juice |
| 1 tbsp. red wine vinegar |
| ¼ tsp. sugar |
| 1 tsp. mustard seeds, crushed |
| ¼ to ½ tsp. hot red-pepper flakes |
| 1 garlic clove, very finely chopped |
| 1 tbsp. olive oil, preferably virgin |

Pour 2 quarts of water into a large pot and add 1 teaspoon of the salt; bring the water to a boil. Cook the broccoli in the boiling water for two minutes. Drain the broccoli and refresh it under cold running water. Transfer the broccoli to a baking sheet lined with a kitchen towel, spreading out the broccoli in a single layer, and let it drain thoroughly.

To make the vinaigrette, whisk together the lemon juice, the vinegar, the remaining ⅛ teaspoon of salt ▶

and the sugar in a small bowl; stir in the mustard seeds, pepper flakes and garlic. Let the mixture stand for five minutes to let the flavors meld. Whisk in the olive oil.

Transfer the broccoli to a serving dish, pour the vinaigrette over the broccoli, and toss it well. Serve the salad immediately.

EDITOR'S NOTE: *You may prepare the broccoli and the vinaigrette up to two hours in advance. Store them in the refrigerator separately, then toss the broccoli with the vinaigrette at serving time.*

sionally, until they are just tender — one hour to one hour and 15 minutes.

While the beans are cooking, put the onions into a heavy-bottomed saucepan with ½ cup of water, 1 tablespoon of the vinegar and half of the sage; bring the mixture to a boil. Reduce the heat and simmer the onions, partially covered, until they are tender and almost all of the liquid has evaporated — approximately 15 minutes.

When the beans have finished cooking, drain them. Drain the potatoes and add them to the beans along with the Canadian bacon, the remaining sage, the salt and some pepper. Gently stir in the onions and ⅓ cup of water. Cover the pot and cook the mixture over low heat, stirring every now and then, until the potatoes are tender and almost all of the liquid is absorbed — approximately 20 minutes.

Transfer the mixture to a large serving bowl and drizzle the remaining 5 tablespoons of vinegar over the salad. Toss the mixture, then add the oil, and toss gently again to coat all of the ingredients with the oil. You may serve the salad hot, at room temperature or chilled.

# Navy Bean and Potato Salad with Onions and Sage

Serves 8
Working time: about 40 minutes
Total time: about 2 hours and 30 minutes
(includes soaking)

Calories **233**
Protein **12g.**
Cholesterol **6mg.**
Total fat **5g.**
Saturated fat **1g.**
Sodium **178mg.**

|  |
| --- |
| ½ lb. dried navy beans, picked over and rinsed |
| ½ lb. pearl onions, peeled |
| 6 tbsp. red wine vinegar |
| 2 tbsp. chopped fresh sage, or 2 tsp. ground sage |
| 1 lb. red potatoes, scrubbed, cut into ¾-inch pieces and covered with water |
| 2 oz. Canadian bacon, diced |
| ¼ tsp. salt |
| freshly ground black pepper |
| 1½ tbsp. olive oil, preferably virgin |

Put the beans into a large, heavy-bottomed pot and pour in enough water to cover them by about 3 inches. Discard any beans that float to the surface. Cover the pot, leaving the lid ajar, and bring the liquid to a boil. Boil the beans for two minutes, then turn off the heat, and let the beans soak for at least one hour.

Drain the beans and return them to the pot. Pour in enough water to cover them by 3 inches. Bring the liquid to a boil. Reduce the heat to maintain a simmer, then cover the pot, and cook the beans, stirring occa-

# Fennel Toast

Serves 8
Working time: about 30 minutes
Total time: about 40 minutes

Calories **88**
Protein **24g.**
Cholesterol **0mg.**
Total fat **3g.**
Saturated fat **1g.**
Sodium **177mg.**

| |
| --- |
| 1 tbsp. olive oil |
| 3 garlic cloves, thinly sliced |
| 1 tbsp. fennel seeds, lightly crushed |
| 2½ cups chopped onion |
| ¼ tsp. salt |
| freshly ground black pepper |
| 2 tbsp. cider vinegar |
| 1 loaf French bread |

Heat the oil in a heavy-bottomed skillet over medium-high heat. Add the garlic and the fennel seeds and sauté them just until the garlic begins to brown — about one minute. Add the onion, the salt and some pepper, and continue cooking, stirring frequently, until the onions are lightly browned — 10 to 15 minutes. Stir in the vinegar and cook the mixture for one minute more. Transfer the onion mixture to a bowl and let it cool slightly.

Slice the French bread into twenty-four ¼-inch-thick rounds; reserve any remaining bread for another use. Spread the rounds with a thin layer of the onion mixture, placing each on a rack as it is finished. Cover the rack with plastic wrap and then set the rack aside until you are ready to bake the prepared bread rounds.

When the fish has finished baking, increase the oven's temperature to 400° F. Uncover the bread rounds and bake them until their edges are lightly browned — about seven minutes. Surround the baked fish with the rounds, or transfer them to a serving plate, and serve them at once.

EDITOR'S NOTE: *These toast rounds are baked on a rack in order to prevent their bottoms from becoming soggy.*

# Fresh Fruit Winter Salad

Serves 8
Working time: about 25 minutes
Total time: about 1 hour and 15 minutes

Calories **107**
Protein **1g.**
Cholesterol **0mg.**
Total fat **0g.**
Saturated fat **0g.**
Sodium **3mg.**

| |
| --- |
| 1 cup fresh orange juice |
| ½ cup dry white wine |
| 1½ tsp. grated orange zest |
| ¼ cup pitted, chopped dates |
| ½ cup raisins |
| 2 crisp apples, preferably Winesap or Stayman, quartered, cored and cut into ¾-inch pieces |
| 1 large pear, preferably Bosc, quartered, cored and cut into ¾-inch pieces |
| 1 cup white, red or black grapes, halved and seeded |

Put the orange juice, wine and orange zest into a heavy-bottomed saucepan. Bring the mixture to a simmer over medium heat and cook it until it is reduced by half — 15 to 20 minutes. Add the dates and the raisins; continue cooking the mixture, stirring occasionally, for three minutes. Remove the pan from the heat.

Place the apple and pear pieces in a large bowl. Pour the hot orange-juice mixture over the fresh fruit and toss the mixture well. Add the grapes and toss the salad again. Refrigerate the salad for 30 minutes. Toss the salad again just before serving.

EDITOR'S NOTE: *This salad will keep in the refrigerator for up to 24 hours. It can be served chilled or at room temperature.*

# Cardamom-and-Ginger Coffee

Serves 8
Working (and total) time: about 15 minutes

Calories **78**
Protein **2g.**
Cholesterol **15mg.**
Total fat **5g.**
Saturated fat **3g.**
Sodium **18mg.**

| |
| --- |
| 7 heaping tbsp. French-roast or other strong roasted coffee beans, ground |
| 2 tsp. ground cardamom |
| 3 tbsp. finely chopped fresh ginger |
| 1 cup whole milk |
| 1½ tsp. sugar |
| ¼ cup heavy cream, well chilled |
| 1 oz. bittersweet chocolate, grated, or 1 oz. semisweet chocolate chips, chopped |

Combine the coffee, 1½ teaspoons of the cardamom, and the ginger; brew this mixture in a coffeepot with 7 cups of cold, fresh water.

While the coffee is brewing, put the milk and sugar into a small saucepan and heat them over low heat, stirring constantly, just until the milk is hot and steaming — about five minutes. When the coffee is ready, pour it and the hot milk into a large, warmed bowl.

In a separate bowl, add the remaining ½ teaspoon of cardamom to the cream and whisk the mixture until it forms soft peaks. Spoon the whipped cream onto the coffee, sprinkle the chocolate on top, and serve.

The tomato-and-orange soup for this spring brunch can be prepared a day ahead of time and chilled. The meringues can be made ahead, too, and stored in an airtight container for several days. Steep the juice for the drink with the rosemary overnight. Prepare all of the salad ingredients and refrigerate them. If you like, the asparagus for the egg noodles can also be prepared the day before the brunch, providing the pieces are tightly covered and chilled.

On the day of the brunch, you can make the seafood sausage up to four hours before poaching it, but be sure to keep it chilled. Prepare the orange garnish for the soup. The fruit for the meringue can be sliced as much as eight hours in advance; fill the meringues just before serving them. Poach the seafood sausage and cook the noodles. Toss the salad just before serving it.

# Cold Tomato-and-Orange Soup

Serves 6
Working time: about 30 minutes
Total time: about 1 hour and 30 minutes
(includes chilling)

Calories **118**
Protein **4g.**
Cholesterol **2mg.**
Total fat **3g.**
Saturated fat **1g.**
Sodium **87mg.**

| |
|---|
| 5 ripe tomatoes (about 2½ lb.), peeled, seeded and cut into large pieces, or 28 oz. canned unsalted whole tomatoes, seeded, the juice reserved |
| 2 scallions, trimmed, the white parts chopped, and the green parts thinly sliced |
| 1 tbsp. fresh lemon juice |
| 2 tsp. olive oil, preferably virgin |
| 2 tsp. honey |
| ½ tsp. curry powder |
| 1 tsp. finely chopped fresh ginger |
| ⅛ tsp. salt |
| freshly ground black pepper |
| 1¼ cups fresh orange juice |
| 1 cup plain low-fat yogurt |
| 1 orange, peeled and segmented, for garnish |

Put the tomatoes and the white parts of the scallions into a food processor or a blender. Add the lemon juice, olive oil, honey, curry powder, ginger, salt and a generous grinding of pepper. Process the mixture until it is smooth. Transfer the mixture to a large bowl and

whisk in the orange juice, the reserved tomato juice if you are using canned tomatoes, and the yogurt. Cover the soup and refrigerate it for at least one hour. To serve, ladle the soup into chilled bowls or cups and garnish each portion with green scallions. Carefully float one or two of the orange sections in each portion.

EDITOR'S NOTE: *This soup may be prepared as much as 24 hours in advance.*

# Scallop and Salmon Sausages with Asparagus and Noodles

Serves 6
Working (and total) time: about 1 hour and 45 minutes

Calories **362**
Protein **23g.**
Cholesterol **96mg.**
Total fat **10g.**
Saturated fat **3g.**
Sodium **330mg.**

| |
|---|
| 2 small carrots, cut into ½-inch pieces (about ½ cup) |
| 3 slices of white bread |
| ⅓ cup low-fat milk |
| 1 egg |
| 1¼ tsp. salt |
| ⅛ tsp. grated nutmeg |
| ⅛ tsp. cayenne pepper |
| 1 salmon steak (about 10 oz.), skinned and boned, the bones reserved |
| ½ lb. sea scallops, rinsed and patted dry, the bright white connective tissue removed and reserved |
| 2 tbsp. fresh lemon juice |
| ¾ cup chopped onion |
| ¾ cup dry white wine |
| 1 lb. asparagus, trimmed and sliced on the diagonal into 2-inch pieces |
| 8 oz. medium egg noodles |
| 2 tsp. unsalted butter |
| freshly ground black pepper |

In a small saucepan, bring 2 cups of water to a boil. Add the carrot pieces and cook them until they are soft — about 10 minutes. Drain the carrots, then refresh them under cold water. Drain the carrots again and set them aside.

Tear each slice of bread into four or five pieces and put the pieces into a food processor. Process the bread until it turns into fine crumbs — about 30 seconds. Pour in the milk, then add the egg, ⅛ teaspoon of the salt, the nutmeg and the cayenne pepper. Process the mixture for about five seconds to combine the ingredients thoroughly.

Add the carrots and process the mixture, using several short bursts of power, until the carrots are ▶

*Cold tomato-and-orange soup is followed by scallop-and-salmon sausages on a bed of spring asparagus and egg noodles, a salad of watercress and peppers, and fruit-filled meringue with a lattice top. Tangerine mimosas are served from a bowl garnished with rosemary and tangerine slices.*

chopped into very small pieces. Transfer the mixture to a bowl, cover the bowl, and put it into the refrigerator to chill. At the same time, put a large, empty bowl into the refrigerator to chill.

Cut the salmon steak into 1-inch chunks and put them, along with the scallops, into the food processor. Process the salmon and scallops until they are finely chopped — about 20 seconds. Transfer the salmon-scallop mixture to the chilled bowl and stir in 1½ tablespoons of the lemon juice. With a wooden spoon, work in the bread-crumb mixture, one half at a time, until the two mixtures are well blended. Cover the bowl and refrigerate it.

To start preparing the sauce, put the reserved salmon bones and the connective tissue of the scallops into a heavy-bottomed saucepan along with the onion, white wine, ⅛ teaspoon of the salt and 1 cup of water. Bring the mixture to a boil, then lower the heat, and simmer the mixture until it is reduced by half — about 20 minutes. Strain the liquid through a sieve into a bowl, gently pushing down on the solids to extract all the liquid; discard the contents of the sieve. Return the strained liquid to the saucepan and set it aside.

While the liquid is reducing, make the sausages. Divide the salmon-scallop mixture in half. Arrange one half in a line near one of the long edges of a piece of plastic wrap about 18 inches long, and form a sausage about 12 inches long, following the technique shown on page 77. Repeat the procedure with the remaining half of the salmon-scallop mixture to form a second sausage.

Pour enough water into a heavy-bottomed, flameproof casserole to fill it 1 inch deep. Bring the water to a boil, then reduce the heat to maintain a low simmer. Put the sausages into the casserole and poach them for 20 minutes, carefully turning them over after 10 minutes. Using two slotted spoons, remove the sausages from the water and set them aside; do not remove the plastic wrap.

While the sausages are poaching, prepare the asparagus and noodles. Bring 8 cups of water to a boil with the remaining teaspoon of salt; add the asparagus pieces and blanch them for one minute. Remove the asparagus with a slotted spoon and set it aside. Add the noodles to the boiling water. Start testing them after five minutes and continue to cook them until they are *al dente*. Drain the noodles and transfer them to a large heated serving platter. Scatter the asparagus over the noodles.

Remove the sausages from the plastic wrap and slice them into ½-inch-thick rounds. Arrange the sausage rounds in several rows on top of the noodles and asparagus. Keep the platter warm while you finish preparing the sauce.

Place the pan containing the sauce over medium heat. Whisk in the butter, along with the remaining ½ tablespoon of lemon juice and a generous grinding of black pepper. When the butter is blended in, pour the hot sauce over the noodles and sausages. Serve the dish immediately.

# Watercress and Red Pepper Salad

Serves 6
Working time: about 15 minutes
Total time: about 20 minutes

Calories **49**
Protein **0g.**
Cholesterol **0mg.**
Total fat **5g.**
Saturated fat **1g.**
Sodium **48mg.**

| |
|---|
| 1½ tbsp. fresh lemon juice |
| 1 tbsp. fresh orange juice |
| 1 tbsp. red wine vinegar |
| ½ tsp. grated lemon zest |
| ⅛ tsp. salt |
| freshly ground black pepper |
| 2 shallots, thinly sliced |
| 2 tbsp. olive oil, preferably virgin |
| 2 sweet red peppers, seeded, deribbed and thinly sliced into 2-inch-long strips |
| 1 bunch of watercress, trimmed, washed and dried |

Whisk together the lemon juice, orange juice, vinegar, lemon zest, salt and some pepper in a large bowl. Add the shallots and let the mixture stand for five minutes so that the flavors can meld. Stir in the olive oil.

Add the pepper strips to the bowl containing the shallot vinaigrette and toss the mixture well. Add the watercress and toss again. Serve the salad at once.

# Strawberry and Kiwi Fruit Meringue

Serves 6
Working time: about 35 minutes
Total time: about 4 hours and 30 minutes
(includes slow baking)

Calories **143**
Protein **2g.**
Cholesterol **0mg.**
Total fat **0g.**
Saturated fat **0g.**
Sodium **28mg.**

| |
| --- |
| *3 egg whites* |
| *¾ cup plus 1 tbsp. sugar* |
| *1 to 2 cups strawberries, hulled* |
| *3 kiwi fruits, peeled and sliced into 6 slices each* |

Line a baking sheet with parchment paper or with a paper bag that has been cut open and flattened. Preheat the oven to 160° F. (If your oven does not have a setting this low, set it just below 200° F.) Keep the oven door propped open with a ball of crumpled foil.

To prepare the meringue, put the egg whites and ¾ cup of the sugar into a large, metal bowl. Set the bowl over, but not in, a pan of steaming water, and whisk the mixture often to dissolve the sugar completely — five to six minutes. Remove the bowl from the heat.

Using an electric mixer, beat the egg whites on medium-high speed until they form stiff peaks and have cooled to room temperature. Transfer the meringue to a pastry bag fitted with a ½-inch star tip.

Holding the tip about ½ inch above the lined baking sheet, pipe out a tightly coiled spiral of meringue until you have formed a disk about 7 inches across. Pipe a single ring of meringue on top of the edge of the disk, forming a low wall that will hold in the fruit filling. On the same baking sheet, pipe an open circle 6 inches in diameter. Pipe three evenly spaced meringue strips across the circle. Pipe three more strips diagonal to the first three to create a lattice pattern.

Bake the meringues until they have thoroughly dried out but are still white — at least four hours. Remove the meringues from the oven and let them cool to room temperature on the baking sheet — they will be quite crisp. The meringues can be made ahead and stored in an airtight container, with a piece of wax paper separating them, for up to two days; in humid weather, however, it is best to use them right away.

Before assembling the meringue, purée ¾ cup of the strawberries with the remaining 1 tablespoon of sugar in a food processor or a blender. Set the berry purée aside. Thinly slice the remaining strawberries and reserve them.

Just before serving, pour the berry purée into the meringue shell. Make a border of the sliced kiwi fruits around the inside of the meringue shell and then arrange the sliced strawberries in a spiral pattern inside the border. Place the lattice top over the fruit-filled meringue at a slight angle. Serve at once.

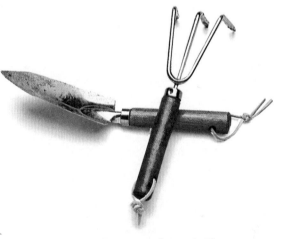

# Tangerine Mimosas

Serves 6
Working time: about 10 minutes
Total time: about 8 hours and 10 minutes (includes chilling)

Calories **141**
Protein **1g.**
Cholesterol **0mg.**
Total fat **0g.**
Saturated fat **0g.**
Sodium **5mg.**

| |
| --- |
| *3 cups tangerine juice or orange juice, preferably fresh* |
| *½ cup white grape juice* |
| *2 sprigs fresh rosemary, or 1 tbsp. dried rosemary* |
| *2 cups chilled dry Champagne* |
| *1 tangerine or orange, thinly sliced into rounds* |

In a bowl, mix the tangerine or orange juice, the grape juice and the rosemary; cover the bowl and refrigerate it for eight hours or overnight to let the flavors meld.

When you are ready to serve, pour the juice into a punch bowl. (If you used dried rosemary, strain the juice into the bowl.) To preserve as much of the Champagne's effervescence as possible, pour it slowly down the side of the punch bowl; float the fruit slices in the punch and serve it in Champagne flutes.

EDITOR'S NOTE: *If you like, place the punch bowl in a larger bowl filled with ice when you are ready to serve the mimosas.*

## SUMMER BRUNCH

*Minted Cucumber Sorbet*
*Summer Salad with Fresh Tuna*
*Peppered Bread Sticks*
*Cherry Summer Pudding*

Most of the work for this summer brunch can be done ahead of time. The bread sticks can be made up to two weeks in advance and then frozen; alternatively, bake them the day before the brunch and, when they have cooled, store them in a sealed paper bag. Prepare the sorbet and the cherry pudding a day beforehand; freeze the sorbet and chill the pudding. The pepper dressing, artichokes, beans, potatoes, tuna and greens for the tuna salad also can be prepared a day ahead and kept separately, covered, in the refrigerator.

On the day of the brunch, unmold the cherry pudding. Dress the greens for the tuna salad and then arrange all of its prepared components. If the sorbet is frozen solid, put it in the refrigerator to soften for 30 minutes before serving it.

## Minted Cucumber Sorbet

THIS PALATE-AWAKENING SORBET GETS
THE BRUNCH UNDER WAY.

Calories **75**
Protein **0g.**
Cholesterol **0mg.**
Total fat **0g.**
Saturated fat **0g.**
Sodium **91mg.**

Serves 6
Working time: about 30 minutes
Total time: 1 to 3 hours, depending
on freezing method

| |
|---|
| *4 large cucumbers* |
| *½ cup sugar* |
| *¼ tsp. salt* |
| *¼ cup cider vinegar* |
| *1 tbsp. chopped fresh mint, or 1 ½ tsp. dried mint* |
| *6 mint sprigs for garnish (optional)* |

Peel, seed and slice two of the cucumbers. Scrub the remaining two cucumbers to rid them of wax and place them in the refrigerator to chill.

In a small saucepan, bring ½ cup of water and the sugar to a boil over medium-high heat and cook the syrup for two minutes. Add the sliced cucumbers, salt and vinegar to the saucepan, reduce the heat to medium and simmer the mixture, stirring frequently, for five minutes. The cucumbers should be translucent. Remove the pan from the heat and stir in the chopped or ▶

*Artichoke wedges form a dramatic garnish for a fresh tuna summer salad, served with red-pepper dressing and peppered bread sticks. Frozen cucumber cups filled with cucumber sorbet, a cherry summer pudding and a pitcher of iced tea complete the brunch.*

dried mint. Purée the cucumber mixture in a blender or food processor and set it aside to cool.

Freeze the purée in an ice cream freezer according to the manufacturer's instructions. (Alternatively, the sorbet can be still-frozen in a shallow pan covered with plastic wrap. Stir the sorbet with a whisk every 30 minutes to break the large ice crystals.)

While the sorbet is freezing, prepare the cucumber cups. Using a vegetable peeler or a channel knife, peel stripes down the length of the cucumbers (technique, page 125). Cut the cucumbers crosswise into thirds, discarding the rounded ends. With a melon baller or a small spoon, scoop out the centers of the cucumber pieces leaving the bottoms intact and ¼-inch of flesh on the sides. Freeze the cups.

Spoon the frozen sorbet into the cucumber cups, mounding it, and return them to the freezer until serving time. If the cups remain in the freezer for more than one hour, allow them to stand at room temperature for about 15 minutes to soften the sorbet slightly. If you wish, garnish each cup with a sprig of mint.

## Summer Salad with Fresh Tuna

THIS UPDATE OF THE CLASSIC *SALADE NIÇOISE* REPLACES THE STANDARD OILY VINAIGRETTE WITH A SPRIGHTLY DRESSING BASED ON ROASTED RED PEPPERS.

Serves 6
Working (and total) time: about 2 hours

Calories **251**
Protein **14g.**
Cholesterol **14mg.**
Total fat **11g.**
Saturated fat **2g.**
Sodium **270mg.**

| |
|---|
| 2 artichokes |
| 1 lemon, halved |
| ¼ lb. fresh green beans, trimmed and cut into 1½-inch pieces |
| ½ cup fresh or frozen peas |
| 6 red potatoes (about 1 lb.), scrubbed |
| ½ lb. fresh tuna (or swordfish) steak, about ½ inch thick |
| ½ lb. assorted salad greens (such as romaine, leaf lettuce, spinach, watercress, endive or radicchio), washed, dried and torn into pieces if necessary |

| |
|---|
| 12 cherry tomatoes, halved |
| 1 small red onion, thinly sliced |
| **Red-pepper dressing** |
| 2 large sweet red peppers |
| 3 tbsp. olive oil, preferably virgin |
| 8 oil-cured black olives, pitted |
| 3 garlic cloves, chopped |
| 6 tbsp. fresh lemon juice |
| ½ cup loosely packed parsley leaves |
| ¼ tsp. salt |
| freshly ground black pepper |

Preheat the broiler. Place the peppers for the dressing about 2 inches below the preheated broiler. Turn them as their sides become slightly scorched. When the peppers are blistered all over, put them into a bowl, cover them with plastic wrap, and set them aside to cool; the trapped steam will loosen the skins.

While the peppers are cooling, trim the artichokes. Cut 1 inch off the tops, snip off the prickly leaf tips with kitchen scissors, then cut off the stems (technique, page 125). Rub the cut edges with a lemon half. Pour enough water into a large, nonreactive saucepan to fill it about 1 inch deep; add the lemon halves and stand the artichokes upright in the water. Cover the pan and bring the water to a boil, then reduce the heat to medium low. Steam the artichokes until a knife slides easily into the stem end and a leaf gently tugged pulls free easily — about 30 minutes. Refresh the artichokes under cold running water and set them upside down on paper towels to drain.

Meanwhile, pour enough water into another large saucepan to fill it 1 inch deep. Set a vegetable steamer in the pan, and put the green beans into the steamer along with the fresh peas, if you are using them. Cover the pan and bring the water to a boil over medium-high heat. Steam the vegetables until they are just tender — about four minutes. Lift the steamer from the saucepan but leave the water in the pan to use again.

Refresh the green beans and the fresh peas under cold running water, then put them into a bowl. If you are using frozen peas, add them at this point. Cover the vegetables with plastic wrap and refrigerate them.

Add water to the saucepan, if necessary, to bring the level back to 1 inch. Replace the steamer, add the potatoes, and steam them until they are tender — about 15 minutes.

To make the dressing, use a paring knife to peel the peppers and slice them open. Remove the stems, ribs and seeds, working over a bowl to catch any juices. Put the peppers into a blender or a food processor along with the pepper juices, oil, olives, garlic, lemon juice, parsley, salt and a generous grinding of pepper. Purée the mixture.

Remove the cooked potatoes from the steamer and let them cool slightly. Cut the potatoes into ½-inch cubes, put them into a bowl, and toss them with ⅔ cup of the dressing. Set the bowl aside.

Preheat the broiler again. Rinse the tuna under cold running water and pat it dry with paper towels. Broil the tuna until its flesh is opaque and feels firm to the touch — about three minutes per side. Cut the fish into ½-inch chunks and toss them gently with the dressed potatoes. Cover the bowl with plastic wrap and refrigerate the mixture.

Cut the artichokes in half lengthwise and remove the hairy chokes with a small spoon or paring knife. Cut each half into thirds.

In a large bowl, toss the greens with all but approximately ½ cup of the remaining dressing; line a large chilled serving platter with them. Arrange the potato-tuna salad, artichokes and tomatoes on the greens, then scatter the beans, peas and onion slices over the top. Pass the remaining dressing as a dip for the artichoke leaves.

# Peppered Bread Sticks

Makes 12 bread sticks
Working time: about 20 minutes
Total time: about 1 hour

Per bread stick:
Calories **111**
Protein **3g.**
Cholesterol **0mg.**
Total fat **1g.**
Saturated fat **0g.**
Sodium **179mg.**

| |
|---|
| 1 envelope fast-rising yeast (about 1 tbsp.) |
| ½ tsp. salt |
| 1 cup unbleached all-purpose flour |
| ¼ cup bread flour |
| ½ tsp. freshly ground black pepper |
| 1 tsp. olive oil |
| 3 tbsp. cornmeal |

Combine the yeast, salt, ¾ cup of the all-purpose flour, the bread flour and the pepper in a large bowl. Heat ½ cup of water and the oil in a saucepan just until they are hot to the touch (130° F.). Stir the hot water and oil into the flour mixture to combine the ingredients thoroughly.

Turn the dough out onto a floured surface and knead in the remaining ¼ cup of all-purpose flour. Continue to knead the dough until it is smooth and elastic — four to five minutes more.

Gather the dough into a ball and place it in a lightly oiled large bowl, turning the ball once to coat it with the oil. Cover the bowl with a damp towel or plastic

wrap and let the dough rise in a warm, draft-free place until it has doubled in bulk — 30 to 40 minutes.

When the dough has risen, punch it down, then transfer it to a floured surface, and knead it for two minutes. Divide the dough into 12 equal pieces. Roll each piece into a 10-inch-long rope.

Preheat the oven to 400° F. Sprinkle a baking sheet with the cornmeal. Lay the dough ropes on the sheet, cover them with the towel or plastic wrap, and let the ropes rise in a warm place for 10 minutes.

Bake the bread sticks until they are dry and lightly browned — 10 to 15 minutes. Transfer them to a rack to cool or serve them at once, piping hot. If you plan to use the bread sticks the following day, store them in an airtight container.

# Cherry Summer Pudding

Serves 6
Working time: about 1 hour
Total time: about 9 hours (includes chilling)

Calories **288**
Protein **6g.**
Cholesterol **0mg.**
Total fat **3g.**
Saturated fat **1g.**
Sodium **256mg.**

| |
|---|
| 4 cups pitted fresh or frozen sweet cherries |
| 6 tbsp. honey |
| 2 tbsp. fresh lemon juice |
| 26 very thin slices white bread, crusts removed |
| 1 cup fresh cherries for garnish (optional) |

Put the 4 cups of fresh or frozen cherries into a nonreactive saucepan. Add the honey and lemon juice to the saucepan; bring the mixture to a boil. Reduce the heat and simmer the cherries for 10 minutes. Purée the cherries in a blender or a food processor.

Spoon enough of the purée into a 1½-quart mold or bowl to coat the bottom. Cover the purée with a single layer of bread, trimming the slices to allow them to fit snugly. Fill the mold with alternating layers of cherry purée and bread, pouring any remaining purée over the last layer. Cover the mold with plastic wrap and put it into the refrigerator for at least eight hours or overnight.

To serve the pudding: Run a knife around the edge of the mold and set an inverted plate over it. Turn both over together and lift off the mold, gently shaking it until the pudding slides out. Garnish the pudding with the fresh cherries if you are using them.

Except for some final steps, all of the work for this autumn brunch can be done a day ahead of time. Make the crepes, the parsley-pepper sauce and the turkey fricassee. Assemble the salad, but do not add the oil, apples, salt and pepper. Combine the mashed sweet potatoes with the sherry and chestnuts so that the dish is ready to bake on the following day. Bake the tart shell and prepare the cranberry filling. Cover everything and store it in the refrigerator overnight.

All that remains to do on the day of the brunch is to bring the crepes to room temperature and then fill them with hot turkey fricassee, bake the sweet potatoes, warm the parsley-pepper sauce, and add the apples, oil, salt and pepper to the salad. To finish the dessert, pour the cranberry filling into the tart shell, arrange the pear slices on top, and bake the tart.

# Apple-Cabbage Salad

Serves 6
Working time: about 20 minutes
Total time: about 25 minutes

Calories **71**
Protein **1g.**
Cholesterol **0mg.**
Total fat **2g.**
Saturated fat **0g.**
Sodium **105mg.**

| |
|---|
| 1¼ lb. green cabbage, shredded or thinly sliced |
| ¼ cup distilled white vinegar |
| 1 tbsp. sugar |
| 1 tbsp. mixed pickling spice |
| 2 red apples, preferably Red Delicious |
| 2 tsp. safflower oil |
| ¼ tsp. salt |
| freshly ground black pepper |

Put the cabbage into a large serving bowl. To make the dressing, put the vinegar, sugar and pickling spice into a small saucepan and bring the liquid to a simmer over medium-high heat; stir the mixture several times to help dissolve the sugar. Simmer the dressing for two minutes. Hold a strainer over the cabbage, then pour the dressing through the strainer. Toss the salad well, then refrigerate it.

When you are ready to serve the salad, quarter and core the apples. Cut each quarter crosswise into thin

*Nestled corn crepes filled with turkey fricassee and topped with parsley-pepper sauce make an attractive main course for this autumn brunch. Mashed sweet potatoes with sherry and chestnuts and an apple-cabbage salad provide seasonal accompaniments. Dessert is a pear and cranberry flan.*

slices. Add the apple slices to the salad along with the oil, salt and some pepper. Toss the salad and serve it immediately.

# Corn Crepes Filled with Turkey Fricassee

Serves 6
Working time: about 35 minutes
Total time: about 1 hour and 15 minutes

Calories **375**
Protein **33g.**
Cholesterol **111mg.**
Total fat **11g.**
Saturated fat **3g.**
Sodium **267mg.**

| |
|---|
| 1½ cups fresh corn kernels (about 2 small ears), or 1½ cups frozen corn kernels, thawed |
| 1¼ cups skim milk |
| 1 egg yolk |
| ⅛ tsp. salt |
| ⅛ tsp. white pepper |
| 1 tbsp. unsalted butter, melted |
| ¾ cup unbleached all-purpose flour |
| ¼ tsp. safflower oil |
| **Turkey fricassee** |
| 1½ lb. turkey breast meat, diced |
| ⅛ tsp. salt |
| freshly ground black pepper |
| 1½ tbsp. safflower oil |
| 1 green pepper, seeded, deribbed and finely chopped |
| 2 onions, finely chopped |
| ½ lb. mushrooms, wiped clean and finely chopped |
| ½ cup dry vermouth or dry white wine |
| ¼ cup unbleached all-purpose flour |
| 1½ cups unsalted chicken stock (recipe, page 138) |
| 1 tsp. fresh thyme, or ½ tsp. dried thyme leaves |
| **Parsley-pepper sauce** |
| 1½ cups unsalted chicken stock (recipe, page 138) |
| 1½ tbsp. cornstarch, mixed with 1 tbsp. water |
| ¼ tsp. freshly ground black pepper |
| ⅛ tsp. salt |
| 2 tbsp. chopped fresh parsley |

To make the crepe batter, put the corn, milk, egg yolk, salt, pepper and butter into a food processor or a blender and purée them. There should be 1¾ cups of the mixture; if there is less, add enough milk to make 1¾ cups of liquid. Transfer the mixture to a bowl and gradually add the flour, whisking until the batter is smooth. Cover the bowl and let it stand for one hour. Alternatively, you may refrigerate the batter, covered, overnight; if the batter has thickened at the end of the refrigeration period, stir in additional milk, 1 tablespoon at a time, until the batter has thinned to its original consistency.

To prepare the turkey fricassee, toss the turkey, the salt and a generous grinding of pepper together in a bowl. Set the bowl aside.

Heat the oil in a large, heavy-bottomed skillet over medium heat. Add the green pepper, onions and mushrooms and cook the mixture, stirring occasionally, until the onion is translucent and the green pepper ▶

is soft — about seven minutes. Add the vermouth or wine, and cook the mixture until almost all of the liquid has evaporated — three to four minutes. Sprinkle the flour over the vegetables, then pour in the stock. Stir the mixture until it is well blended. Add the turkey and the thyme, then reduce the heat, and simmer the mixture, partially covered, until the turkey firms up and turns white, indicating that it is cooked through — about four minutes. Remove the skillet from the heat; keep it warm while you prepare the sauce.

To make the parsley-pepper sauce, bring the stock to a simmer in a small saucepan. Stir in the cornstarch mixture, pepper and salt, and simmer the liquid for six minutes. Stir in the parsley, then cover the sauce, and keep it warm while you prepare the crepes.

Heat a 6-inch crepe pan or nonstick skillet over medium-high heat. Add the ¼ teaspoon of oil and spread it over the entire surface with a paper towel. Pour about 2 tablespoons of the crepe batter into the hot pan and immediately swirl the pan to coat the bottom with a thin, even layer of batter. Pour any excess batter back into the bowl. Cook the crepe until the bottom is set — about one minute. Lift the edge with a spatula and turn the crepe over, then cook the crepe on the second side until it too is set — 15 to 30 seconds. Slide the crepe onto a warmed plate; cover the crepe and keep it warm. Repeat the process with the remaining batter, brushing the pan lightly with more oil if the crepes begin to stick. Transfer the cooked crepes to the plate as you go, separating them with pieces of wax paper. There should be 12 crepes in all.

Place about 4 tablespoons of the filling in a line down the center of a crepe and roll the crepe to enclose the filling. Transfer the filled crepe to a warmed serving platter. Repeat the process with the remaining crepes and filling. Spoon the warm parsley-pepper sauce over the crepes and serve them at once.

# Mashed Sweet Potatoes with Sherry and Chestnuts

Serves 6
Working time: about 20 minutes
Total time: about 1 hour

Calories **263**
Protein **5g.**
Cholesterol **1mg.**
Total fat **3g.**
Saturated fat **0g.**
Sodium **135mg.**

| |
|---|
| ½ lb. fresh chestnuts |
| 2 lb. sweet potatoes (yams), peeled and cut into 1-inch slices |
| 1½ cups skim milk |
| ¼ tsp. salt |
| ⅛ tsp. white pepper |
| 2 tsp. safflower oil |
| 1 tsp. finely chopped shallots |
| ¾ cup dry sherry |

Lay a chestnut with its flat side down on a cutting board. Using a sharp paring knife, make an *X* in the rounded side of the shell, cutting through both the shell and the inner skin. Repeat the process with the other chestnuts. Cook the chestnuts in boiling water for 10 minutes. Remove the pan from the heat but do not drain the chestnuts. Alternatively, bake the chestnuts in a 350° F. oven on a baking sheet until the cut shell begins to curl — about 15 minutes.

While the chestnuts are still warm, remove the shells and as much of the brown skin as possible. (Waiting until the chestnuts are cool would make them difficult to peel.) Finely chop the chestnuts and set them aside.

Preheat the oven to 350° F.

Pour enough water into a saucepan to fill it 1 inch deep. Set a steamer in the pan and put the sweet potatoes into the steamer. Bring the water to a boil, and steam the sweet potatoes, covered, until they are tender — about 10 minutes. Transfer them to a bowl.

Pour the milk into a saucepan and bring it just to a simmer. Add the milk to the sweet potatoes. Mash the sweet potatoes until they form a smooth purée, then stir in the salt and white pepper.

Heat the oil in a small, heavy-bottomed skillet set over medium-high heat. Add the shallots and cook them until they are translucent — about one minute. Stir in the chopped chestnuts and the sherry; simmer the mixture until the sherry has reduced by half — about three minutes. Combine this mixture with the sweet potatoes, then transfer them to a baking dish. Smooth the surface of the purée with a spatula. Bake the sweet potatoes until they are heated through — about 15 minutes. Serve at once.

# Pear and Cranberry Flan

Serves 6
Working time: about 25 minutes
Total time: about 1 hour

| | |
|---|---|
| Calories **244** | 1 cup sifted unbleached all-purpose flour |
| Protein **3g.** | 2 tsp. sugar |
| Cholesterol **10mg.** | ¼ tsp. salt |
| Total fat **7g.** | 2 tbsp. cold unsalted butter, cut into pieces |
| Saturated fat **3g.** | 1 tbsp. cold unsalted margarine, preferably corn oil, cut into pieces |
| Sodium **112mg.** | ½ tsp. pure vanilla extract |
| | 3 cups cranberries, picked over |
| | ¼ cup fresh orange juice |
| | 5 tbsp. sugar |
| | 3 ripe but firm pears, peeled, cored, cut into ¼-inch-thick slices and tossed with the juice of ½ lemon |
| | 1 tbsp. chopped filberts (optional) |

To prepare the flan pastry, combine the flour, sugar and salt in a food processor or a bowl. If you are using a food processor, add the butter and margarine and cut them into the dry ingredients with several short bursts. With the motor running, slowly pour in the vanilla and 3 tablespoons of cold water, blending the dough just until it begins to form a ball. If you are making the dough in a bowl, use a pastry blender or two knives to cut the butter and margarine into the dry ingredients, then mix in the vanilla and water with a wooden spoon or your hands. Shape the dough into a ball and wrap it in plastic wrap. Chill the dough until it is firm enough to roll — about 20 minutes.

Meanwhile, put the cranberries into a small sauce-

pan with just enough water to float the berries; bring the liquid to a simmer and cook the cranberries until they burst — about four minutes. Drain the cranberries to remove any excess liquid and put them in a blender or food processor; add the orange juice and 3 tablespoons of the sugar. Process the cranberries just until they are puréed. (Take care not to overprocess the cranberries. Crushing the seeds can make the purée bitter.) Strain the purée through a fine sieve to remove the seeds and skins; chill the purée.

To form the flan shell, set the chilled dough on a floured surface. Using a rolling pin, flatten the ball of dough into a round, then roll the dough into a 10-inch circle. Transfer the dough to an 8-inch tart pan with a removable bottom, rolling the dough around the rolling pin and then unrolling it onto the tart pan. Gently press the dough into the corners and up the sides of the tart pan. Fold any excess dough back into the pan and press it well into the sides. Chill the flan shell for 10 minutes.

Preheat the oven to 425° F.

To prebake the flan shell, put the tart pan on a baking sheet. Prick the bottom of the dough several times with a fork. Line the flan shell with a round of wax paper and fill it with dried beans; this helps the pastry keep its shape. Bake the pastry for 10 minutes, remove the beans and wax paper, and continue baking until the flan shell is dry and just begins to color — about five minutes more. Remove the shell from the oven and let it cool in the tart pan.

Meanwhile, make a sugar syrup: Heat the remaining 2 tablespoons of sugar with 2 tablespoons of water in a small saucepan over medium-low heat until the sugar is dissolved — three to four minutes.

To assemble the flan, fill the bottom of the cooled flan shell with the cranberry purée. Arrange the pear slices on top in a circular pattern, overlapping the pieces slightly. Brush the pears and the edge of the pastry with the sugar syrup. Sprinkle the top with the filberts if you are using them. Bake the flan until the pears are soft and glazed — about 10 minutes. Remove the flan from the tart pan and serve it hot or cold.

## BUFFET BRUNCH

*Pork Loin with Cider and Rosemary*
*Scrambled Eggs with Smoked Salmon in Toast Cups*
*Whole-Wheat Biscuits with Bulgur and Citrus*
*Pear Butter (recipe, page 49)*
*Pancake Torte with Spinach and Onion Filling*
*Broccoli Gratin*
*Riesling-Simmered Apricots and Pears*
*with Yogurt Cream*

Make the pear butter *(recipe, page 49)* for this buffet brunch up to one week in advance. The pancakes can be made a day or two ahead. The day before the brunch, marinate the pork, cook it, and reduce the sauce to a glaze. Make the dessert and refrigerate it. Store everything in the refrigerator, covered well.

On the day of the brunch, make the broccoli gratin; the gratin can sit for up to one hour, covered, after it is baked. Bring the dessert and the meat to room temperature. Make and chill the dessert topping and bake the biscuits. Make the spinach-onion filling and fill the pancake; cover it with foil and then heat it in a 325° F. oven for about five minutes. Cook the rutabaga and put it on a warmed platter; arrange the sliced meat on the rutabaga, cover the platter with foil, and heat it in the oven with the pancake for about 10 minutes. Warm the glaze. If you like, heat the dessert for 15 minutes at 200° F. to warm it. Make the mocha coffee.

# Pork Loin with Cider and Rosemary

Serves 12
Working (and total) time: about 50 minutes

Calories **224**
Protein **22g.**
Cholesterol **64mg.**
Total fat **9g.**
Saturated fat **2g.**
Sodium **110mg.**

| |
|---|
| 1 tbsp. safflower oil |
| 2¾ lb. boneless pork loin roast, trimmed of fat |
| 1 small onion, coarsely chopped |
| 1½ tbsp. fresh rosemary, or 1 tsp. dried rosemary |
| ¼ tsp. salt |
| freshly ground black pepper |
| 4 cups apple cider or unsweetened apple juice |
| 3 tbsp. cider vinegar |
| 2 lb. rutabagas, peeled and coarsely grated (about 5 cups) |
| 3 fresh rosemary sprigs for garnish (optional) |

Heat the oil in a large, heavy-bottomed skillet over medium-high heat. Put the pork into the skillet and brown it lightly on all sides — about seven minutes in all. Add the onion, rosemary, salt and some pepper to the skillet; pour in the cider or apple juice and bring the mixture to a boil. Reduce the heat to medium low, cover the skillet with the lid ajar, and simmer the pork for 10 minutes. Turn the meat over and continue simmering it, partially covered, until the juices run clear when it is pierced with the tip of a sharp knife — about 10 minutes more. Remove the pork from the skillet and keep it warm.

Add the vinegar to the skillet and simmer the cooking liquid over medium-high heat until it is reduced to about ⅔ cup — 15 to 20 minutes.

While the sauce is reducing, pour enough water into

a large saucepan to fill it about 1 inch deep. Set a vegetable steamer in the pan and put the rutabagas into it. Cover the pan, bring the water to a boil, and steam the rutabagas until they are tender — about three minutes. Drain the rutabagas, pressing them lightly with the back of a spoon to release any excess liquid. Transfer the rutabagas to a large serving platter and keep them warm.

Cut the pork into ⅛-inch-thick slices and arrange the slices on top of the rutabagas. Strain the sauce over the pork slices and, if you like, garnish the platter with the rosemary sprigs. Serve at once.

*A loaded sideboard awaits guests: Pork loin on a bed of rutabaga is served with squares of broccoli gratin, wedges of spinach-filled pancake torte, wheat biscuits with pear butter, scrambled eggs with salmon in toast-and-lettuce cups and, for dessert, Riesling-simmered apricots and pears.*

# Scrambled Eggs with Smoked Salmon in Toast Cups

CUTTING DOWN ON THE NUMBER OF EGG YOLKS USED
REDUCES THE CHOLESTEROL IN THIS RECIPE.

Serves 12
Working (and total time): about 30 minutes

Calories **115**
Protein **7g.**
Cholesterol **72mg.**
Total fat **5g.**
Saturated fat **1g.**
Sodium **233mg.**

| |
|---|
| 1 head Boston lettuce, or ⅓ lb. radicchio |
| 12 slices whole-wheat bread, crusts removed |
| 3 eggs, plus 6 egg whites |
| ⅛ tsp. salt |
| freshly ground black pepper |
| 2 tbsp. olive oil, preferably virgin |
| 2 garlic cloves, finely chopped |
| ¾ cup diced sweet red pepper |
| 2 oz. smoked salmon, finely chopped (about ¼ cup) |
| 5 scallions, trimmed and thinly sliced |
| 1 tbsp. fresh lemon juice |

Separate the lettuce or radicchio leaves and wash them if necessary. Set the leaves aside. Preheat the oven to 400° F. and lightly oil a muffin pan.

Using a rolling pin, flatten each slice of bread slightly. Gently press one slice of bread into each muffin cup. Bake the bread until it is crisp and lightly browned — 10 to 15 minutes. Keep the toast cups warm.

Whisk together the eggs, egg whites, salt, some pepper and 1½ tablespoons of the oil in a large bowl. Heat the remaining ½ tablespoon of oil in a large, nonstick skillet over medium-high heat. Add the garlic and red pepper and cook them for one minute, stirring constantly. Add the salmon, scallions and lemon juice; cook the mixture for two minutes more. Pour in the egg mixture and cook it, stirring constantly, just until the eggs are set but still moist — about two minutes.

Spoon the scrambled eggs into the toast cups, place each toast cup on a lettuce leaf, and serve at once.

# Whole-Wheat Biscuits with Bulgur and Citrus

Makes 16 biscuits
Working time: about 25 minutes
Total time: about 40 minutes

*Per biscuit:*
Calories **80**
Protein **3g.**
Cholesterol **1mg.**
Total fat **2g.**
Saturated fat **0g.**
Sodium **67mg.**

| |
|---|
| ¼ cup bulgur |
| 1 cup plain low-fat yogurt |
| 2 tsp. grated orange zest |
| 1 tsp. grated lemon zest |
| 2 tbsp. safflower oil |
| 1½ cups whole-wheat flour |
| 3 tbsp. sugar |
| 1½ tsp. baking powder |
| ⅛ tsp. salt |

Put the bulgur into a bowl and pour in ⅓ cup of boiling water. Cover the bowl and let the bulgur stand until it is tender — about 15 minutes.

Preheat the oven to 375° F. Lightly oil a baking sheet or line it with parchment paper.

Drain the bulgur thoroughly, put it into a large bowl, and stir in the yogurt, orange zest, lemon zest and oil. Sift the flour, sugar, baking powder and salt over the bulgur mixture and stir them together just until they are combined. The dough will be quite sticky.

Turn the dough out onto a heavily floured surface. Dust your hands and the top of the dough with flour. Flatten the dough with your hands until it is about ¼ inch thick, using flour as needed to keep the dough from sticking. Using a 2½-inch-round cookie cutter, cut out as many biscuits as possible and put them on the baking sheet. Press the scraps of dough together and use them to make more biscuits.

Bake the biscuits until they are lightly browned — 15 to 20 minutes. Serve the biscuits hot.

# Pancake Torte with Spinach and Onion Filling

Serves 12
Working (and total) time: about 25 minutes

Calories **88**
Protein **4g.**
Cholesterol **25mg.**
Total fat **4g.**
Saturated fat **1g.**
Sodium **106mg.**

| |
|---|
| 2 lb. fresh spinach, stemmed and washed, or 20 oz. frozen spinach, thawed |
| 2 tsp. olive oil, preferably virgin |
| 2 onions, thinly sliced |
| 1 tbsp. fresh thyme, or 1 tsp. dried thyme leaves |
| ⅛ tsp. salt |
| freshly ground black pepper |
| ⅓ cup cider vinegar |
| **Pancake batter** |
| ¾ cup unbleached all-purpose flour |
| ⅛ tsp. salt |
| 1¼ cups low-fat milk |
| 1 egg, plus 1 egg white |
| 1½ tbsp. olive oil, preferably virgin |

To make the pancake batter, sift the flour and salt into a large bowl. In another bowl, whisk the milk, egg, egg white and oil together. Pour the milk mixture into the dry ingredients, stirring just until the batter is blended; do not overmix. Set the batter aside while you make the filling.

If you are using fresh spinach, cook it in 3 quarts of boiling water for one minute, then drain it and run cold water over the spinach to refresh it; thawed frozen spinach does not require cooking. Squeeze the spinach in your hands to extract as much water as possible and coarsely chop it.

Heat the oil in a large, heavy-bottomed skillet over medium heat. Add the onions, thyme, salt and some pepper, and cook the mixture, stirring occasionally, until the onions are translucent — about 10 minutes. Increase the heat to medium high and continue cooking the onions, stirring frequently, until they have browned — five to 10 minutes more. Pour in the vinegar and continue to cook the onions until all the vinegar has evaporated — one to two minutes. Stir the spinach into the onions and cook the mixture for one minute. Keep the spinach mixture warm while you cook the pancakes.

Heat an 8-inch skillet or griddle (box, page 55) over medium heat. Pour in half of the pancake batter and swirl the skillet or griddle to distribute the batter over the bottom. Cook the pancake until the underside is golden — two to three minutes. Turn the pancake and cook it until the second side is lightly browned — two to three minutes more. Transfer the pancake to a plate and keep it warm while you make a second pancake with the remaining batter.

Spread the spinach filling over the first pancake and top it with the second pancake. Cut the pancake torte into 12 wedges and serve the wedges either warm or at room temperature.

EDITOR'S NOTE: *The pancakes for this torte can be made up to two days in advance and kept in the refrigerator, covered with plastic wrap. On the day of the brunch, make the filling and spread it between the pancakes. Cover the torte with foil and heat it in a 350° F. oven for about five minutes.*

# Broccoli Gratin

Serves 12
Working time: about 25 minutes
Total time: about 1 hour and 15 minutes

Calories **76**
Protein **6g.**
Cholesterol **35mg.**
Total fat **4g.**
Saturated fat **2g.**
Sodium **135mg.**

| |
|---|
| 2 lb. broccoli, the florets separated from the stems, the stems peeled and cut into ½-inch pieces |
| ½ cup low-fat milk |
| 1 cup part-skim ricotta cheese |
| ¼ cup light cream |
| 1 egg, plus 1 egg white |
| ¼ cup freshly grated Parmesan cheese |
| 2 garlic cloves, finely chopped |
| ¼ tsp. grated nutmeg |
| ¼ tsp. salt |
| freshly ground black pepper |

Preheat the oven to 350° F.

Pour enough water into a large saucepan to fill it about 1 inch deep. Set a vegetable steamer in the pan, bring the water to a boil, and put the broccoli stems into the steamer; cover the pan and steam the stems for three minutes. Add the broccoli florets and steam the florets and stems until both are tender — about five minutes more. Remove the steamer from the saucepan and refresh the broccoli under cold running water; drain it thoroughly.

Put the broccoli into a food processor and pour in the milk; process the broccoli in short bursts until it is coarsely puréed. (Do not overprocess — the mixture should not be smooth.)

In a large bowl, whisk together the ricotta, cream, egg, egg white, 2 tablespoons of the Parmesan cheese, the garlic, nutmeg, salt and some pepper. Mix the broccoli purée into the ricotta mixture.

Spoon the broccoli mixture into an 8-by-12-inch baking dish; sprinkle it with the remaining 2 tablespoons of Parmesan cheese. Bake the broccoli gratin in the oven until it is firm and lightly browned — 35 to 40 minutes. Cut the gratin into 12 squares or diamonds, arrange them on a large plate and serve them at once.

# Riesling-Simmered Apricots and Pears with Yogurt Cream

Serves 12
Working time: about 30 minutes
Total time: about 1 hour and 15 minutes
(includes chilling)

Calories **131**
Protein **2g.**
Cholesterol **10mg.**
Total fat **3g.**
Saturated fat **2g.**
Sodium **9mg.**

| |
|---|
| 1½ cups Riesling or other dry white wine |
| ¾ lb. dried apricots |
| 3 ripe pears (about 1¼ lb.), peeled, cored and cut into ¾-inch pieces |
| **Yogurt cream** |
| ⅓ cup heavy cream |
| ¼ cup plain low-fat yogurt |
| 1 tbsp. confectioners' sugar |
| ½ tbsp. pure vanilla extract |

Combine the wine and apricots in a large, nonreactive saucepan and bring the wine to a simmer over low heat. Simmer the mixture, stirring occasionally, until the apricots are soft and the liquid is reduced to about ½ cup — about 15 minutes.

Drain the apricots in a sieve set over a bowl, gently pressing them with a spoon to extract as much liquid as possible. Transfer the apricots to another bowl and set them aside. Pour the liquid back into the saucepan, add the pears, and cook them over low heat, stirring occasionally, until they are soft — about 20 minutes. The liquid should be syrupy. Line an 8-inch cake pan with a round of wax paper or parchment paper.

Add the pears with their liquid to the apricots and gently stir them together. Spoon the mixture into the prepared pan and spread it evenly over the bottom. Chill the fruit until it is firm — about 45 minutes.

Meanwhile, beat the cream until it forms soft peaks; mix in the yogurt, sugar and vanilla just until they are blended. Spoon the cream into a bowl and chill.

When the dish is set, run a knife around the edge of the pan and invert a serving plate on top of it. Turn both over together; lift away the pan and peel off the paper. Serve the dessert warm or at room temperature topped with the yogurt cream.

# Techniques

## Shaping Pot Stickers

**1** MOISTENING THE WRAPPER. Lay a dumpling wrapper on the work surface; keep the other wrappers under cloth or in their container to prevent dehydration. Place a heaping teaspoonful of filling on the wrapper. Moisten a fingertip and run it along half of the wrapper's rim.

**2** PLEATING THE RIM. Pick up the wrapper with its filling and pinch the top of the moistened and unmoistened rims together. Then gather two or three pleats on each side of the dumpling and press to seal the edge.

**3** CURLING THE CRESCENT. To give a sharper crescent shape to the pot sticker, curl back its ends and pinch them between your fingers, as shown. Set the pot sticker aside on a lightly floured surface, covered with a damp cloth, and form the other pot stickers in the same manner.

## Forming Buns

**1** FILLING THE BUN. After making the dough rounds as directed in the recipe on page 98, set one before you on the work surface. Place a heaping teaspoon of the prepared bean filling onto the center of the round.

**2** SHAPING THE BUN. Pick up the round and its filling and gather up the sides with your fingers. Enclose the filling by simultaneously pinching and twisting the edges together. Set the bun aside and proceed to fill and form the other buns in the same manner.

## Preparing Artichokes for Summer Salad with Fresh Tuna

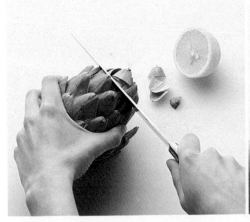

**1** *TRIMMING THE TOP. With a stainless-steel knife, cut off about 1 inch of the top of an artichoke. To prevent discoloration, rub the trimmed edges with a freshly cut lemon.*

**2** *SNIPPING THE LEAF TIPS. Trim off the hard, prickly tips of the outer leaves with kitchen scissors. Use the knife to cut off the stem of the artichoke near the base of the globe. Rub the trimmed edges with lemon. Repeat steps 1 and 2 with the other artichoke. Cook and cool the artichokes as directed in the recipe. Slice them in half lengthwise.*

**3** *REMOVING THE CHOKE. Hold a half in the palm of one hand and use a small, sturdy spoon to dig out the choke — the inedible, furry center. Discard the choke and slice the half into thirds for the salad. Repeat the procedures for the other three halves.*

## Carving Cucumber Cups

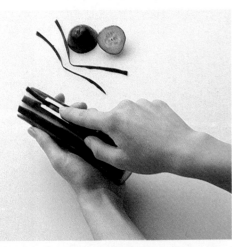

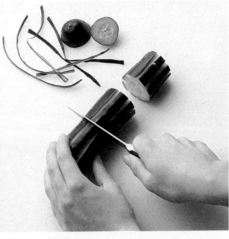

**1** *REMOVING THE ENDS. With a sharp knife, cut off the ends of a cucumber. Holding the cucumber firmly in one hand, use a citrus stripper (shown here) or vegetable peeler to score the peel lengthwise at intervals of about half an inch.*

**2** *DIVIDING THE CUCUMBER. Lay the scored cucumber on the work surface, and use the knife to divide it into three cylindrical segments of the same length.*

**3** *MAKING CUPS. Using a melon baller (shown here) or a small, sturdy spoon, scoop out a segment, leaving about ¼ inch of flesh on the sides and a thicker bottom. Scoop out the remaining two segments, then repeat the procedures with the other cucumber.*

3
Brown bread with walnuts and apricots takes only eight minutes to bake in the microwave oven (recipe, opposite).

# Microwaved Breakfasts

The microwave oven truly comes into its own in the morning, when the minutes that it shaves from conventional cooking times are especially important to the hurried cook. Seven of the recipes in this section constitute a selection of quick-and-easy breakfast and brunch dishes — breads; fruit and vegetable dishes; and bran muffins that can be prepared, from start to finish, in just 10 minutes. And as a bonus, there are two recipes for preserves that can help brighten up a breakfast; they cannot be beaten for color and freshness, but unlike regular jams and jellies, these have to be stored in the refrigerator. Most of the recipes in this section require less than half an hour overall time, and in no instance does the necessary working time exceed 30 minutes.

The abbreviated cooking process offers a number of advantages in addition to convenience. Not only does microwaving help preserve natural color, shape and texture; it also ensures that fewer nutrients are destroyed. And when fruits and vegetables are cooked in the microwave oven, they essentially cook in their own juices, with only a little additional liquid needed. As a result, fewer of the heat-sensitive and water-soluble vitamins and minerals are destroyed or drawn out of the food.

The microwave process cannot brown the surface of breads and bars: They ordinarily emerge from the oven looking unappealingly pallid when white flour is used. Thus whole-grain products are called for here; the brown bread on page 127 and the raisin and nut spreads on page 137 owe their appetizing appearances to well-chosen ingredients, which also have the advantage of furnishing fiber, vitamins, minerals and protein appropriate to a healthful morning meal.

All of the recipes have been tested in both 625-watt and 700-watt ovens. Since power settings often vary among ovens made by different manufacturers, the recipes use "high" to indicate 100 percent power, "medium high" for 70 percent and "medium low" for 30 percent.

## Brown Bread with Walnuts and Apricots

Serves 10
Working time: about 15 minutes
Total time: about 30 minutes

Calories **157**
Protein **4g.**
Cholesterol **0mg.**
Total fat **2g.**
Saturated fat **0g.**
Sodium **158mg.**

| |
|---|
| ½ cup dried apricots |
| ½ cup buttermilk |
| ½ cup molasses |
| 1 egg white |
| 1 cup whole-wheat flour |
| ½ cup cornmeal |
| 2 tbsp. dark brown sugar |
| ¼ tsp. salt |
| 1 tsp. baking soda |
| ¼ cup chopped walnuts |

Put the apricots into a glass measuring cup and pour in ¼ cup of water. Microwave the apricots on high for two minutes.

In a bowl, mix together the apricots, buttermilk, molasses and egg white. In another bowl, stir together the flour, cornmeal, brown sugar, salt, baking soda and walnuts. Stir the flour mixture into the apricots to combine them.

Lightly oil a 9-by-4-inch glass loaf pan and spoon in the batter. Put a glass pie plate upside down in the microwave oven; set the loaf pan on it. (This is not recommended for ovens with rotating turntables.) Microwave the loaf on medium (50 percent power) for eight minutes, rotating the dish a quarter turn every two minutes. If areas of the bread start to overcook, shield them with small pieces of aluminum foil. Check the bread for doneness by inserting a wooden pick or a cake tester into the center; if it comes out clean, the bread is done. Set the loaf pan on a rack and let the bread cool in the pan for 10 minutes before unmolding and slicing it.

# Prunes with Orange, Pineapple and Kiwi Fruit

Serves 6
Working (and total) time: about 30 minutes

Calories **89**
Protein **1g.**
Cholesterol **0mg.**
Total fat **0g.**
Saturated fat **0g.**
Sodium **2mg.**

| |
|---|
| 1 lb. dried pitted prunes, quartered (about 2 cups) |
| 1½ tsp. cornstarch |
| ⅓ cup fresh orange juice |
| 3 tbsp. honey |
| ½ tsp. pure vanilla extract |
| 1 orange |
| 5 oz. fresh pineapple, cut into 1-inch wedges (about 1 cup) |
| 1 kiwi fruit, peeled, halved and cut into 12 pieces (six pieces per half) |

Put the prunes and 2½ cups of hot water into a bowl. Cover the bowl and microwave it on high until the water simmers — about four minutes. Remove the bowl from the oven and let the prunes stand, covered, for 10 minutes.

Meanwhile, combine the cornstarch and the orange juice in a bowl, then stir in the honey and the vanilla extract. Cook the mixture on high until it thickens — about two minutes.

Using a sharp, stainless-steel knife, cut off both ends of the orange. Stand the orange on end and cut away vertical strips of the peel and pith. Slice the orange into ¼-inch-thick rounds. Cut the rounds in half.

Drain the prunes and put them into a bowl with the orange, pineapple and kiwi fruit. Pour the honey mixture over the fruits and stir them together gently. Microwave the fruit mixture on high for one minute and 30 seconds to heat it through. Serve the fruit warm.

## Bran Muffins with Dates

Makes 6 muffins
Working time: about 5 minutes
Total time: about 10 minutes

| | |
|---|---|
| Calories **205** | ½ cup pitted chopped dried dates |
| Protein **5g.** | ½ cup cake flour |
| Cholesterol **2mg.** | ½ cup whole-wheat flour |
| Total fat **4g.** | ¾ cup wheat bran |
| Saturated fat **1g.** | ⅛ tsp. salt |
| Sodium **238mg.** | ¾ tsp. baking soda |
| | 1 cup plain low-fat yogurt |
| | ¼ cup molasses |
| | 4 tsp. safflower oil |

Mix the dates with 1 teaspoon of the cake flour and reserve them. Combine the remaining cake flour, the whole-wheat flour, bran, salt and baking soda in a bowl. Add the yogurt, molasses and oil, and stir gently until all of these ingredients are combined. Fold the dates into the batter.

Line the cups of a microwave muffin pan with baking papers or lightly oil six ½-cup ramekins. Divide the muffin batter among the cups or ramekins. Cook the muffins on high for about three minutes, turning the muffin pan or rearranging the ramekins halfway through the cooking time. Test the muffins for doneness every 30 seconds by inserting a wooden pick in their centers; when the pick comes out clean, remove the muffins from the oven. Let the muffins stand for five minutes before serving them.

# Fig Coffeecake
## with Chutney Sauce

Serves 10
Working time: about 15 minutes
Total time: about 35 minutes

Calories **152**
Protein **3g.**
Cholesterol **1mg.**
Total fat **3g.**
Saturated fat **0g.**
Sodium **161mg.**

| |
|---|
| 1½ cups unbleached all-purpose flour |
| ¼ cup sugar |
| 2 tsp. baking powder |
| 1 tsp. curry powder |
| ¼ tsp. salt |
| ⅔ cup skim milk |
| 2 tbsp. safflower oil |
| 1 egg white |
| ½ cup coarsely chopped dried figs (about 3 oz.) |
| grated zest of 1 lemon |
| **Chutney sauce** |
| ½ tbsp. cornstarch |
| ¾ cup apple cider or unsweetened apple juice |
| 2 tbsp. mango chutney |
| ¼ cup golden raisins |

Combine the flour, sugar, baking powder, curry powder and salt in a bowl. Add the milk, oil and egg white to the dry ingredients and stir them together just until blended. Gently mix in the figs and the lemon zest.

Lightly oil a 5-cup glass or plastic ring mold. Spoon the batter evenly into the mold, smoothing the top of the batter with the back of the spoon. Tap the mold several times on the counter to release any air bubbles from the batter.

Microwave the cake on medium high (70 percent power) for about eight minutes, rotating the cake a one-third turn twice during the cooking time. When the cake is done, a wooden pick or a cake tester inserted into the center will come out clean. Remove the cake from the oven and let it cool.

While the cake cools, combine the cornstarch and cider or apple juice in a small bowl and stir the mixture to dissolve the cornstarch. Add the chutney and raisins and microwave the mixture on high until the sauce has thickened — about two minutes. Remove the sauce from the oven, stir it, and let it stand until cool.

Unmold the coffeecake onto a serving plate, slice it, and serve with the sauce.

# Cranberry Jelly

Makes 2 cups
Working time: about 10 minutes
Total time: about 8 hours (includes chilling)

*Per tablespoon:*
Calories **23**
Protein **0g.**
Cholesterol **0mg.**
Total fat **0g.**
Saturated fat **0g.**
Sodium **0mg.**

| |
|---|
| 12 oz. cranberries (about 2½ cups), picked over |
| ¾ cup sugar |
| 1 tbsp. liquid pectin |

Put the cranberries into a 2-quart glass bowl with 1 cup of water and microwave them on high, uncovered, for six minutes.

Work the cranberries through a sieve set over a bowl and discard the contents of the sieve. Add the sugar to the bowl and stir the mixture. Microwave the cranberry mixture on high for eight minutes, stirring midway through the cooking time. Remove the bowl from the oven, stir in the pectin, and let the jelly cool.

Spoon the jelly into a jar, and cover and chill it overnight. Cranberry jelly can be kept up to two weeks covered and stored in the refrigerator.

# Tangerine Marmalade

Makes ¾ cup
Working time: about 10 minutes
Total time: about 2 hours and 30 minutes
(includes cooling)

*Per tablespoon:*
Calories **57**
Protein **0g.**
Cholesterol **0mg.**
Total fat **0g.**
Saturated fat **0g.**
Sodium **0mg.**

| |
|---|
| 3 tangerines (about ½ lb.) |
| ⅛ tsp. pure vanilla extract |
| ¾ cup sugar |

Remove the peel from the tangerines and chop it finely. Put the chopped peel into a measuring cup. Juice the tangerines and strain the juice into the measuring cup; add the vanilla and stir the mixture well. If necessary, add enough water to measure 1 cup.

Pour the tangerine mixture into a bowl and microwave it, uncovered, on high for five minutes. Stir in the sugar and microwave the bowl on high for five minutes more. Stir the mixture and then microwave it for three minutes more. Test the marmalade for consistency by dropping a spoonful of it onto a chilled plate (*technique, right*). Let the marmalade cool for one minute and then push it gently with your fingertip; it should wrinkle slightly as you push it. If the marmalade fails to wrinkle, microwave it for one minute more and then test it again; be careful not to overcook the marmalade or it will become too thick.

Let the marmalade cool to room temperature before serving it — about two hours. The marmalade can be stored in the refrigerator for up to two weeks.

EDITOR'S NOTE: *If the marmalade thickens during refrigeration, you can thin it by microwaving it, uncovered, on high for one minute. Stir in 2 tablespoons of water and microwave it on high for two minutes more; then allow it to cool.*

## Obtaining a Proper Jell

TESTING THE MARMALADE. *Drop a spoonful of the marmalade onto a flat plate that has been well chilled. Let the syrup cool for a minute, then slowly push a finger across it. If done, the marmalade should wrinkle slightly. If not, microwave the syrup for another minute and test again.*

# Pork and Spinach Pie

Serves 6 as a main course
Working time: about 30 minutes
Total time: about 1 hour

Calories **299**
Protein **22g.**
Cholesterol **83mg.**
Total fat **11g.**
Saturated fat **4g.**
Sodium **571mg.**

| |
|---|
| 10 oz. package of frozen chopped spinach |
| 8 oz. pork tenderloin, trimmed of fat and finely chopped |
| 1 tsp. fennel seeds |
| 2 garlic cloves, finely chopped |
| 1 tsp. ground coriander |
| ⅛ tsp. salt |
| 1 tbsp. olive oil, preferably virgin |
| ½ tsp. hot red-pepper flakes |
| 2½ cups buttermilk |
| 1 egg, plus 1 egg white |
| 1 loaf French bread (about ½ lb.), cut into ½-inch-thick slices |
| ½ cup freshly grated Parmesan cheese |

To thaw the spinach, set the package on a plate and microwave the spinach on high for two minutes and 30 seconds. Set the spinach aside.

In a bowl, mix together the pork, fennel seeds, garlic, coriander, salt, ½ tablespoon of the oil and ¼ teaspoon of the red-pepper flakes. In another bowl, mix the buttermilk, the eggs, the remaining ½ tablespoon of the oil and the remaining ¼ teaspoon of red pepper.

Spread the bread slices in a single layer on the bottom of a baking sheet with shallow sides. Pour all but ¼ cup of the buttermilk mixture over the bread, then turn the slices. Let the bread stand, turning the slices frequently until they have absorbed nearly all the liquid — about 15 minutes.

Microwave the pork mixture on high for one minute and 30 seconds, stirring the mixture once at midpoint. Remove the spinach from the package and squeeze it with your hands to remove as much liquid as possible. Stir the spinach into the pork mixture, along with the reserved ¼ cup of the buttermilk mixture and about half of the cheese.

Spoon about one quarter of the pork mixture into an 11-inch glass pie plate. Arrange half of the bread slices in a close-fitting layer on top of the pork. Cover the bread with half of the remaining pork mixture and top this layer with the remaining bread. Spread the remaining pork mixture on top of the bread and pour over any of the buttermilk mixture remaining on the baking sheet. Cover the dish with plastic wrap.

Microwave the dish on medium (50 percent power) for four minutes. Rotate the dish halfway and cook it another four minutes. Uncover the dish and scatter the remaining cheese over the top. Cook the dish eight minutes more. Let the dish stand for at least five minutes before serving it.

# Spaghetti Squash with Basil and Pine Nuts

Serves 6
Working time: about 10 minutes
Total time: about 40 minutes

Calories **106**
Protein **3g.**
Cholesterol **1mg.**
Total fat **3g.**
Saturated fat **0g.**
Sodium **78mg.**

| |
|---|
| 1 spaghetti squash (about 4 lb.) |
| ¼ cup unsalted chicken stock (recipe, page 138) or water |
| 1 ripe tomato, peeled, seeded and cut into small dice |
| ¼ cup chopped fresh basil |
| 2 tbsp. pine nuts, toasted in a small, dry skillet over medium heat |
| 2 tbsp. freshly grated Parmesan cheese |
| 1 tsp. fresh lemon juice |
| 1 tbsp. sugar |
| 1 whole basil leaf for garnish (optional) |

Pierce the squash several times with the point of a sharp knife. Put the squash into a shallow casserole and microwave it on high for 20 minutes, turning it over halfway through the cooking. Remove the squash from the oven and let it stand for 10 minutes.

Cut the squash in half lengthwise; remove and discard the seeds. Using a fork, remove the flesh of the squash and put it into a bowl. Add the stock or water, tomato, chopped basil, pine nuts, Parmesan cheese, lemon juice and sugar and toss them all together. Microwave the mixture on high for four minutes. Remove the squash from the oven and let it cool slightly. Put the squash into a serving dish and garnish the dish with the basil leaf, if you are using it. Serve the squash at once.